MW00611561

9/11
The Unknown Reality
of the World

Communications from Seth on the
Awakening of Humanity ~ Volume One

9/11
The Unknown Reality
of the World

Casandra Smith
&
Mark Frost

Seth Returns Publishing
San Rafael, California

Copyright © 2004 Seth Returns Publishing
First Printing

Published by Seth Returns Publishing
P.O. Box 150152
San Rafael, CA 94915-0152
(415) 459-2487

Editorial: Casandra Smith and Mark Frost
Cover Art, Design, Typography & Layout: Mark Frost
Printed by: Hayes Printing & Publishing

All rights reserved. No part of this book may be reproduced in any form or by any electronic or mechanical means, including photocopying, recording, or information storage and retrieval systems, without permission in writing from the publisher, except by a reviewer, who may quote brief passages in a review.

Library of Congress Cataloging-In-Publication
CIP   2003105803

ISBN 0-9740586-0-2
Printed and bound in the U.S.A.

A portion of the proceeds of the sale of this book

will be used to help feed the hungry people

of the world.

CONTENTS

Introduction by Cas.................................*xv*
Introduction by Mark..........................*xxiii*
Introduction by Seth............................*xxxi*
Understanding the Seth Entity...............*xxxv*
Preface...*xli*

CHAPTER 1

THE CONTRACT OF LIFE 1
    Making the Transition
    The Contract and Learning From the Loss
    Suicide
    Guilt
    Negative Energies
    Exercise: The Box

CHAPTER 2

THE SOUL'S EVOLUTION
    YOU ARE ALL ONE.........................27
    The Soul's Reality
    Evolution of Race
    Exercise: Speaking to Strangers
    Cultures

Hate and Anger
Moving Forward
Exercise: Working Through
Your Thoughts and Beliefs

CHAPTER 3

EVOLVING AS A SPECIES 41
Responsibility for Your Actions
The Danger Zone
Free Will - Natural Impulses
Your Point of Power - Now
Exercise: Point of Power

CHAPTER 4

MOVING OUT OF THE DARKNESS
OF A WORLD IN TURMOIL..........................55
Corporate Greed and Globalization
Global Collapse
Aligning Your Energy
Opening Your Minds
Exercise: Healing the Nation

CHAPTER 5

THE REALIGNMENT OF BELIEF SYSTEMS
AND THE AWAKENING OF HUMANITY.....71
Tolerance of Other's Beliefs
Questioning the Mass Belief Systems

CONTENTS

Exercise: Analyzing Your Mind/
Thought Beliefs
The Beliefs of Your Leaders
Other Planetary Life Forms
Re-scripting Your Future

CHAPTER 6

THE MISUSE OF RELIGION FOR THE
REPRESSION OF HUMANITY......................89
Religious Beliefs
Man's God
God is You
The Manipulation of Spiritual Truths

CHAPTER 7

CHANGING THE CONSCIOUSNESS
OF MANKIND.................................103
You the Creator
Communicating with Others
Thought Health and The Evolution of DNA
Exercise: Opening the Chakras
Spiritual Knowledge

CHAPTER 8

THE REALITIES OF A DISTORTED WORLD........119
Surrendering Your Power
The Cult's Inception

Exercise: Ray of Light
Idealists and Fanatics
One of the Leaders

CHAPTER 9

THE FORCES OF POWER.......................................131
The Negative Media
Government and Man's god
Religion and Government
The Western World Government
Terror and Fear

CHAPTER 10

THE MULTIDIMENSIONAL REALITY
OF THE SOUL...147
Simultaneous Lives
Simultaneous Lives Diagram
Other Selves and Other Realities
Your Inner Reality
Exercise: Healing Your Other Selves
Your Life Plans
Thought Reality
Ego vs. Soul and Soul Validation
The Walls of Separation

Epilogue: The Acceptance of Self..........169

Glossary..175

Questions and Answers with Seth..........181

INTRODUCTION BY CAS

As I write this introduction I know that I have been awakened from the cosmic slumber I have resided in for the majority of my life. Like many of those around me, I was caught up in life's daily encounters, never giving much thought to what my beliefs were or why I had them. But all of that started to change after 9-11. In the aftermath of those events I was left with an intense feeling of vulnerability within the borders of a country I once believed to be invincible. I couldn't understand how this could have happened because like others I wasn't paying attention.

My story begins when my sister sent me a book on past lives. I enjoyed reading this material and began to wonder what I might have done in a past life. Wouldn't it be interesting to see what I had accomplished or not accomplished? I also hoped that in some past life I could discover the reason why I couldn't get myself motivated to do my art. I have artistic talent and we had just finished constructing a studio for me to work in yet I was not painting. I figured that if I could get to the root of the problem I could make some progress in my painting, so I found a Hypnotherapist and made an appointment. During my first hypnosis session I experienced what seemed to be a life in the 1920's and the death that ended that existence. Toward the end of the session, I felt myself surrounded by peaceful warmth and I was acutely aware of an energy presence, as though there was someone there with me in spirit form. That session lasted about three hours. Then during the second session something happened that changed my life forever. I became aware of my soul and the unbelievable bliss that surrounds it. The intense love was so powerful that I began laughing with joy. Since then I have had many positive changes in my life. I now know that life is just an experience and that death is not to be feared.

While in a euphoric state towards the end of the second session, I began to speak in a different language. I found out later it was called Sumari. At first I had no idea what I was saying, seemingly answering questions and asking them as well. Some time into it I perceived my own thoughts also coming out in Sumari. I was stunned by this, having never learned any other language in this life but English. Since then I have sung songs in Sumari and have been able to speak this language whenever I choose, though it usually occurs during meditation. I have been told that in Sumari there is a wealth of information available to me to give to others and that I should focus on learning how to translate it. Because I don't know of any others who speak this language this may be a difficult project, however I am determined to give it a try.

All during this time I had the feeling that I was being guided to these experiences. I became curious about my soul-self and began meditating daily, always going to that favorite place, in between lives. While in this state I began having lengthy conversations with someone and one day I finally asked him to tell me his name. He identified himself as Seth. Such an ordinary name, I thought to myself. I thought I would be communicating with someone with a more cosmic name.

At the time, I was still looking for a Hypnotherapist in my area to continue the past life regressions. Mark had a unique ad in the phone book and so I gave him a call. (I was later to find out that Seth had actually arranged this meeting.) I met Mark at his office and had my first couple of sessions. I didn't want to tell him right away about Seth. I wanted to make sure that he was open-minded enough to hear it. Then on the day of our third session I was shopping for a book on how to increase my psychic abilities. Since I was communicating with this entity, I thought I should try to develop some better skills. I picked up a book on the subject matter and then out of habit turned to the back pages to see what other books the author recommended. And there it was: *Seth Speaks*. My heart was pounding. Could this be my Seth? I immediately looked for the recommended book and there on the shelf in front of me I found it: *Seth Speaks*. My hands were shaking as I picked up the book. I became even more nervous as I read his short introduction and realized that I had tapped into something that I might not be ready for.

You see, throughout my life I have been heavily conditioned to stay within the boundaries of conservative thinking. It seemed each time I tried to break free, someone would rope me back in. So taking a risk, I bought the book, got into my car and began reading. As I scanned the pages, I noticed that these ideas were similar to what Seth had been saying to me. It made me all the more curious, wondering to myself, who is this guy and why have I never heard of him? *Seth Speaks* was written back in my hippie days and I figured I should have at least heard something about him. But then again, I wasn't "awake" back then. I wasn't in the habit of reading this type of material. (Incidentally, Seth has confirmed to me that there were other reasons why I was not exposed to his material in those days.)

That afternoon I met with Mark and asked him if he had ever heard of Seth. Mark said he had heard of him and asked me if I could bring him forward in hypnosis. So we began that session bringing forth Seth. Mark was apparently very familiar with the Seth material and he proceeded to ask all of the appropriate confirming questions. The Seth that I had been talking to was indeed coming through under hypnosis, talking through me and identifying himself as the same Seth who had written many books years ago. We soon discovered that Seth was quite good at conveying his messages and he was interested in writing about the events of 9-11. Now, I enjoy doing the hypnosis as I find it quite relaxing, but here I was going to have this entity or energy personality as he calls himself speaking through me? This was very frightening to me yet also very interesting. I felt that I had to keep an open mind about it and decided that if he wished to say something then at least we should listen and write it down.

For the first few sessions with Mark, I went through the hypnotic procedure convinced that this was a necessary step to get me relaxed, but soon found out that Seth had other ideas. Seth told me we would do a session and while under hypnosis I would open my eyes and try to stay focused. And it worked. I was able to open my eyes and Seth continued talking. I remember this eye-opening session so well. It was as though I was sitting on the side of myself as Seth began to scan the room and make his observations. It was such an odd feeling to be both in and out of the room. We did a couple more sessions and then one day Seth told me we didn't need the full hypnotic procedure. He said, "You can do it." The next session I was prepared to lie down again but Seth just came through and opted for the chair. From that time on I sat in a chair and Seth communicated to Mark face-to-face.

Much of the information Seth dictated to Mark I do not remember. I could hear him speak, but it was if I was in an echo chamber hearing a louder, deeper version of my voice. I would get a fuzzy feeling in my eyes and Mark would look somewhat out of focus. Then I knew Seth was present. In the beginning, I experienced many different sensations that I came to find out later were all part of Seth's adjustments to make the contact with me easier. It was an awkward feeling knowing that someone else was sharing my space with me. Often he would talk to me throughout the day, sometimes at night when I was resting and listening to him and even in the dream state. I felt as though large blocks of information were being filtered into my brain, information that I never would have been able to conceive of with my extremely limited knowledge of this subject matter.

Since Seth has entered my life, many of my barriers have been broken down. I have been opened up to other dimensions of reality and have known a deep inner peace. I can now look at my fellow humans with a greater understanding of our intimate relationships with each other on this planet. Currently, Seth has begun dictating another book through me. There is a vast amount of knowledge that he wishes to give to humanity and as long as he keeps speaking I will do my best to pass it along.

INTRODUCTION BY MARK

During my final few weeks in graduate school I had a lot on my plate: struggling to put together a final paper so that I could indeed graduate, continuing to counsel a full caseload of clients at the school and trying to drum up business for my private hypnotherapy practice. I was looking forward to taking a few weeks off after graduation and maybe go to Maui with my girlfriend Carol or just hang out at the house and relax. But when a woman contacted me and said she would like to do some "past lives" work, I was intrigued. I was eager to strengthen my skills in this popular subspecialty of hypnotherapy. The woman made an appointment for the next week and we met at my office. This new client had a sparkle in her eye and an active sense of humor. She also had an aura of familiarity about her that puzzled me. We had an initial session and hit it off immediately. She seemed to anticipate my questions and I hers and in a couple of sessions we developed a rapport, as though we had been working together for some time. Looking back, I have to say that there was something other-worldly about those first meetings in my cramped but cute little office. It sounds like a cliché but it's true: I didn't know it then, but my life was about to take a dramatic, mind-bending turn.

Shortly before our third session my new client phoned me and asked, "Have you ever heard of Seth? I'm receiving communications from someone who calls himself Seth." I almost dropped the phone in shock but I replied nonchalantly something like, "Yes, I know a little about Seth." I felt as though I had something to protect. Seth was a valuable part of my private life as a seeker, as a student of the healing arts. I had studied the Seth material for many years and like some of his more dedicated readers, I guarded that relationship fiercely. But here I suspected someone was playing a prank on me. It seemed somehow impossible that this fellow would be speaking again after all these years and speaking through a client of mine, no less. It just looked like a setup. Nonetheless, excited but doubtful, I made an appointment to do another regression with my client and attempt to contact this spirit who claimed he was Seth.

And to my amazement, the third session with my new client became the first Seth session. From my home library I brought a few of my favorite Seth books and placed them on my office bookshelf, to make him feel at home if he were indeed to make an appearance. My client arrived and I turned on the video camera to document the proceedings. I relaxed my new client and inducted her with some traditional hypnotic suggestions while she rested on the couch. Unbelievably, twenty minutes into the session, she "found" Seth and in a few moments he was speaking through her on a variety of subjects. I was, to put it mildly, impressed. I felt like jumping up and gleefully hopping around the office like a little kid, making strange noises as they do. This appeared to be the Seth who dictated *Seth Speaks* and other famous texts. His energy was palpable and filled the room. His love for humans and his sense of humor was evident and he kidded me good-naturedly throughout the hour and a half session. Somehow I had the presence of mind to ask a few probing questions, testing to see if this was an elaborate hoax or some sort of psychological anomaly. I asked if he was the Seth who spoke through a woman who first communicated with him through a Ouji board. My client as Seth answered in the affirmative, with a pleasant smile. I asked several pointed questions about his creative endeavors with his first subject and her husband. He gave me immediate, specific replies suggesting that he knew what he was talking about. Some of the material was information I had never heard before and this certainly was not information my new client could have known. She claimed to know nothing of the Seth material and I believed her. And she was hypnotized after all, exhibiting the classic physical signs of the hypnotic state. For a large part of the session, Seth discussed some local public health matters and gave me instructions on how to begin to resolve them. I was in an altered state myself as I struggled to contain the enormity of this, the implications of this experience.

In the next few sessions, Seth planned his return to publishing after what he called his "sabbatical" of 18 years. The new material would serve to "enlighten the minds" of readers, assisting them on their unique paths of learning in this chaotic era. Seth prepared us for our adventure by putting the book material "into our heads" as we slept. We also were able to communicate with him throughout the day telepathically if we wished. Cas is a natural at this but it took me a few weeks to pick out his voice from my chorus of internal dialogues. I finally succeeded and was quite gratified to "hear" Seth's eloquent answers to my pitifully mundane questions on business and personal matters.

Now I know this probably sounds like it's time to call community mental health on Mark and bring him in for an evaluation, but consider this: I have just completed five years of academic instruction and training in psychology. I can identify the classic syndromes and I know what mental illness looks like, at least what we currently label as mental illness, and this is not mental illness. On the contrary, what I am experiencing is mental functioning at its healthiest, though admittedly at its rarest. This is the peak of mental health. Yet I would not be completely honest if I were to claim that there were no episodes of psychic whitewater. It is a confrontational challenge to the ego, so enamored with consensus reality, to as Seth suggests, "just open up to the multidimensional existence of your soul." That's a tall order, at least for me, though I am gradually getting better at it. At times I feel as though I am coming undone, and this may be a good thing. The psychic armor is cracking and falling away. I'm becoming a great deal more open and accepting. In a way, it's like extending your peripheral vision until you can see behind you. Seth's exercises help us to exercise our soul's perception, allowing us a glimpse of the unknown reality.

So Seth has returned and it appears that he is going to stay awhile and write some books, though possibly not in the identical style that made him famous and this may cause some concern. I don't feel the need to comment on this new creative tack he has taken other than to say I'm enjoying it and learning from it more and more as I read and absorb the material. As is always the case with Seth's work, at least it seems to me, the material speaks for itself. Of all the "philosophical" reading I've done his has the loudest ring of truth and I've heard countless other readers comment similarly. Curious readers can compare his prose in 9/11 with other works printed more than twenty years ago. The same metaphors are there, the same cadence, the same subtle wit. And though he has spoken with an ardent flare, his current message is much more urgent. *Book written 2004*

Seth wanted me to tell the reader that he has returned to restate the facts-of-life for us so that we will not make critical mistakes that may doom our planet. This first book is a primer - a basic text - thus the powerful little exercises sprinkled throughout. His subject is the soul's evolution and the crucial importance of love, personal responsibility and positive intention in the moment to further this process. I encourage you the reader to immerse yourself in the information - the light - presented here. Let it wash over you and see and feel if it is opening you up, reminding you of something splendid that you may have forgotten, reminding you of some unfinished business in your soul's journey.

As for me, it seems I've graduated into a totally new livelihood, completely alternative and that suits me perfectly. All plans for going on vacation and cultivating some sort of normalcy at home have gone out the window yet I am quite grateful and honored for this new development in this life, in this timeframe. And now as I look back, events that did not make sense to me before are beginning to become clear. I can see the sequence, the long chain of choices made in countless moment points that led to this collaboration across dimensions. And maybe it is there, at some point in simultaneous time, where we all can meet to share our personal adventures with this material now that he has returned. I urge you to make that connection. There is strength in numbers and the time is upon us to create our finest, most loving expression of our unique embodied souls.

****

Some of the practical matters involved in this collaboration may be of interest to readers and so I include them here. I transcribed Seth's dictations into a word processing program on my computer as he spoke through Cas. I also videotaped all sessions held in my office and later used these tapes to cross-check my transcription. We agreed with Seth that for the sake of clarity and flow of material, we would publish this work without the addition of notes and comments. I think that Seth's fine prose style comes through quite well in this format. We are continually fine-tuning our procedures to allow Seth's words to be transcribed and published in the exact form he wished them to be. MF

INTRODUCTION BY SETH

Let me start by introducing myself. I am the energy personality essence known as Seth and I am no longer focused in the physical realms of the third-dimensional world that you call Earth. Many of you will remember some or all of the many works that I wrote through my first subject. The time has come for me to speak again. It has been many of your Earth years since I have penned any works through one of my human counterparts. I reside in the higher dimensions where there is no time or space as you know it. My form is of etheric matter. I am again presenting some basic truths that you have forgotten, to you, the reader, whom I cannot see. However, as I acknowledge your existence, sight unseen, I would ask that you allow me the same. This material is written to give the reader insights into your reality and stimulate you to question the beliefs and values that you hold. I am making no particular gender distinction when I write in the masculine sense, as soul knows no gender. It is used to encompass all, as this is your language and I will stay within that framework. I am communicating with a different portion of my energy from a different timeframe as you understand it, to facilitate these transmissions to you than I did with my first subject, however all writings are telepathically given by me in much the same manner that I used with him. This material has been delivered through another extension of the Seth energy personality in this timeframe that you are focusing on who goes by the name of Casandra Smith. My desire in this writing was to keep this material formatted as simple as possible, for time as you understand it is coming to a close in this chapter of the evolution of mankind. I have chosen to include the words "God" and " The Creator" which refer to the energy source from which all life is created on your planet. It is the energy source that moves through every living thing in your world. I wish to use language that is more familiar to your understanding of this infinite energy within the broadest spectrum of your societies. These writings do not support or deny any religious groups within the framework of your existence. In the Glossary of the back of this book I will clarify the terms I have used for a clearer understanding.

The awakening of mankind into the unity of consciousness dimension is imminent. The events of 9-11 left many souls on this planet in a state of confusion. Some of that confusion will be eliminated as one reexamines the reality of your world. As always, you have free will to do as you wish in the evolution of your soul. I hope to give you the reader a greater understanding of your nature and the impending shift of the planet and its citizens into the fourth dimension. I wish to make some of the unknown realities a reality to you and show you how to use the powers of your thoughts, beliefs and actions to heal the consciousness of mankind. I am as real as you are, and in reading this material I wish to express my fondest love for you all and hope that what you read will lift you to new dimensions of awareness, bring you into focus with who you are and help you in your understanding of the events of 9-11.

UNDERSTANDING
THE SETH ENTITY

There seems to be some confusion as to who I am so I will endeavor to bring a clearer understanding to this phenomenon. One must first begin to look at the Seth entity as a whole. We are a vast and intricate entity communicating at various points in consciousness throughout the multitudinous universes. To begin, I am the same entity that communicated with my first subject yet I am that and more. There are portions of me that are communicating with you that were not present in my earlier communications and vice versa. As you begin to understand that the Seth entity as a whole is responsible for the transmissions and not just one aspect of it, you will start to get a greater understanding of yourself and the vastness of YOUR multidimensional nature.

The name Seth is the communication waveband that we use to interact with humans and other life forms. It is our signal so to speak. There are very few individuals in human form who are able to tune into this frequency due to their particular mental makeup. Since the beginning of time we have been communicating with humans on various levels. My communications with you and Cas are from certain aspects of the greater whole. As I communicate from this aspect of the entity I do not do so singularly but as part of the whole. My function is to bring forth the information from the whole of the entity. For instance, to help you further understand what I mean, let us take you as an example. You would not consider your fingers or toes separate from you, yet they move independently from your hands and feet. They are aspects of your physical structure and part of the whole. Just as all the organs of your body function simultaneously and independently for the survival of the whole, so it is with the entity known as Seth. For those of you who understand this you may see Seth as a channel. It is a channel for communication and it contains the harmonics and vibrations attuned to its specific wavelength to allow for communication.

We are not of the extraterrestrial nature. One cannot tune into the Seth channel unless one is part of the Seth entity itself. This is where some of the confusion has been. There are many extraterrestrials as you call them communicating with humanity at this time. These entities communicate on a universal channel so to speak and anyone who knows how to tune into this waveband can access communication telepathically with them. The Seth entity however is not of this waveband. Our highly specialized network of communication is done within the vastness of the entity itself, for we operate on many dimensional-levels in many solar systems. In order to understand that in itself, one must first have a comprehension of dimensions and multi-universality. For this reason there are not vast numbers of humans in communication with the Seth entity. It is necessary to keep the information from being highly distorted, as it would be if it were to be communicated as the extraterrestrials do. When a portion of the entity is ready, then the communication can begin. With Cas, this portion of the entity had all the components in place and we began transmission. I am an aspect of the same Seth that communicated with my first subject and yet as I said I am more because of Cas' personality structure and mental framework. There are other portions of self involved that were not needed with my earlier subject, yet we are the same.

So just as you as a whole understand your physical oneness yet can see its independence, so it is with the whole of you. You are made up of a vast network of selves all contributing to the whole of you, which I am trying to make you aware of. You are like a finger or toe in the makeup of your greater self. And to take that one step further, your greater self is like a finger or toe of another greater self, which eventually connects to the greater self of All That Is. The Seth entity in its vastness is just a minute part of the energy of All That Is. There has been much confusion as to who I am and when Seth communications are present in your everyday lives through these transmissions. Many of you are still clinging to the idea that since my first subject transcended the physical form that I have ceased to exist as well. Neither he nor myself have ceased to exist and neither will you when you no longer have use for your physical body.

I am still my previous subject's teacher as he is part of the entity yet we are separate aspects of the entity. I continue our communications with Cas at this time since this aspect of the entity was ready and is still in physical form. There is still much to reveal to humanity and that is why I am once again producing books. Although you may find some differences in language it is because this portion of the entity (Cas) does not have the extensive vocabulary that my earlier subject had, however that does not mean that there is less validity to the transmission.

As in all transmissions and over-shadowings, the host body and mind will still filter information through its own vocabulary. I am able to communicate quite proficiently through Cas and have managed quite well to convey my thoughts without confusing the reader. The complexity of the information alone is quite a task to reveal due to your own limitations as to the greater understanding of self and your conditioning, which we will endeavor to undo.

PREFACE

The disturbed energies of a fear-driven society
have been taken for granted in your everyday life...

Human beings have been reluctant over the centuries to tune into the telepathically transmitted information that is being given to them. They have essentially put on their cosmic blinders in favor of old superstitious ways. The fear of the unknown has kept their awareness locked in the dark recesses of their minds, pushed aside like leaves on the pathway. They choose to ignore many of the messages that would enable them to complete their soul's evolution. Locked in the grip of fear and anger they flounder around like fish out of water looking for answers to their dilemma. They are besieged with an abundance of negative stimuli from the media. They are then flocking like geese to the nearest psychoanalyst to explain to them why they feel the way they do. Often they are given prescriptions for a variety of medications and sent on their ways. In this great mass of circular logic they rotate in and out of their perceived dilemma until the overload of their behavior finally gets the best of them through disease or illness. The medical profession has taken it upon itself - as is quite fashionable these days - to label these anomalies with syndromes of every type imaginable. Then the patient walks out of the medical office with the assumption that he or she has a justifiable condition and therefore can again push aside the inner voices of their own consciousness for a more narrow-minded answer to their problems. They can then continue on their self-destructive path and be fully justified in doing so. They no longer have to confront their behavior and its source. They merrily take their pills and go on about their daily business. Meanwhile their symptoms once again are pushed aside. This endless circle of behavior eventually catches up to them and they find themselves with another physical malady and so it goes, on and on, one episode after the other. The disturbed energies of a fear-driven society have been taken for granted in your everyday life. The majority tenaciously cling to these ideas and refuse to accept any other explanations that are not grounded in scientific beliefs.

If you would learn to surround yourselves with
The Creator's light and energy, you would essentially
be able to eradicate the constant barrage of fears
that have surrounded you...

Many of you have adopted destructive sets of beliefs, lives filled with ego-gratification, greed and selfishness. This however is not the soul's true nature. If left alone without all of the negative stimuli, the soul would return to a peaceful hum that it has always known. Mankind would be in sync with Mother Earth and the rest of the planetary life that dwells in your dimension. If you would learn to surround yourselves with The Creator's light and energy, you would essentially be able to eradicate the constant barrage of fears that have surrounded you. Love and light, which is knowledge, are the only things that are needed to free you from your path of self-destruction. They will dissolve the layers of negativity like acid on ripe fruit and release your soul's essence from its spiritual slumber. The soul's essence of each and every one of you is trying to pry itself free from the grip of the negative energies surrounding your existence.

Many of you have already been awakened from your spiritual slumber and are diligently participating in moving the rest of mankind into the arena of awareness. Now when I am referring to negative influences or energies, I would clarify here what I am attempting to convey. It is with respect to your ability to allow your ego's desires to control your vehicle instead of your soul's light, as the soul only knows its light and love. It also refers to certain energies in and around your planet that do not serve to evolve with the plan of The Creator.

As you perceive your reality as something that You have created, then you can and will change it for the better. To find oneself, one must look within, for within lies the perfection of God and the Universe that is ultimately - You. Eventually all of you will see the light, if not now then later. For the entities that refuse to evolve and continue on their greedy, self-centered path with no regard for their fellow man, you may find yourself removed from the humming rhythms of the evolving Earth's move into the peaceful fourth dimension and assigned to one of the lower-vibrational, two-dimensional planets until such time as your soul yearns to move towards the light and be cleansed. Like a stone encased inside a mountain, there you will sit and wait until you have had enough time to seek the love light. Now I am not trying to be gloom and doom here, for those entities that are relinquished to this dimension do not in any way reflect the majority of you. Most of you will start soon to get the messages and move towards the light. However, for those of you who persist in the cat-and-mouse game of dominating everyone and everything on the planet, your evolution will not be forthcoming as swiftly as the rest of your planet's citizens and you may be left behind. I have spoken before about how you can change your reality with your thoughts. Since your reality IS your thoughts, this will not be hard to do.

The writings in the following chapters are to prepare mankind for the impending shift of consciousness on your planet and to help you in questioning your beliefs, analyzing your thoughts and opening up your minds to your greater reality. As you awaken you will be opened to a new spiritual kind of existence - a unity with the rest of mankind - and released from your spiritual slumber. A mass continuity of consciousness is about to unfold and the belief systems of the world are in the dawn of an unprecedented historical change.

Many years ago I told you there would be the coming of the third personality of The Christ trilogy. The Christ trilogy consisted of three beings: John the Baptist, Jesus Christ and Paul or Saul as he was also known. Saul and the Jesus Entity have already entered your world as members of your planet's Spiritual Hierarchy and are teaching among you along with several others. However, due to certain systems of probabilities on your planet, The Christ Entity himself has also emerged in your world today as a man. This personality will form a new psychic entity. This entity is now preparing to emerge fully into your world as prophesied as the "Second Coming" of the Christian religion.

That entity as I said will not be coming at the end of your world as you have greatly distorted it, but to guide humanity in your world now. He has returned to set up a new system of thought, to reawaken humanity to its relationships with each other and to realign Christianity as it has greatly distorted the spiritual ideas that were originally to be implemented for the evolution of humanity. He has come into your world as a World Teacher and with him he brings many members of your planet's Hierarchy that will help in the restructuring of your world. He comes as a multi-dimensional personality and will not be oriented in terms of one sex, one color or one race. He will manifest himself at will in many different forms thus exhibiting the multidimensional nature of his being. He will clearly reveal methods enabling each individual to be intimately in contact with their own being and that of The Creator. He will be guiding humanity to use those inner senses of their true spiritual nature and recognize the multidimensional nature of their reality. As humans evolve their awareness, they will be confronted with their actions and memories of all their lives. A great realignment of the relationship with your souls and with each other will be revealed to all. This is happening now and he will soon emerge publicly and reveal himself.

CHAPTER 1

The Contract of Life

Making the Transition | The Contract & Learning from
the Loss | Suicide | Guilt | Negative Energies |
Exercise: The Box

*They are not gone, they simply have moved on
in their soul's evolution...*

Making the Transition

You are energy. All of your soul essence is formed of energy and that energy can never be terminated. It changes from one form to the other as you move in and out of life experiences. Your soul essence is eternal and ageless. God, Buddha, Allah, The Christ or whatever terminology You wish to use to describe the energy of The Creator, is alive in all creations and cannot be destroyed. When you think of the souls who perished in 9-11 or any event for that matter, they did not really perish at all, they simply moved from one form of energy to another. They are not gone, they simply have moved on in their soul's evolution.

Remember here that I am presenting this information to you as simple as possible, as there is a much greater depth to all of this...

The physical vehicle is but a materialized form which the soul uses on the physical plane for expression and evolution. It is tailored to the vibrational-coordinates of a third-dimensional perspective of reality. Within this system of reality it is made and re-made many times through reincarnational journeys as the soul seeks to evolve itself. This materialized form of energy is limited to its vibrational rate within your system and appears to the human eye as solid, dense and quite real, yet in other systems it would appear quite transparent. Its energy is interchangeable and within the framework of the third dimension appears to its recipient as the basis for all life experience. Remember here that I am presenting this information to you as simple as possible, as there is a much greater depth to all of this, but it must be written in your terms for you to understand.

Because of mankind's preconceived notions of his physical mortality he has oftentimes assumed that his physical vehicle is all there is. The soul however, is piloting this craft and with its inherent knowledge of itself and its own wisdom it is fully capable of re-grouping its energy when faced with imminent crisis to the physical vehicle. All souls when facing a horrific death, will exit the body before the moment of impact. No soul wishes to remain during such an event. When the souls have exited the body they are fully aware of the events taking place but without the physical trauma. The dimension they will reside in is very similar to yours as it is a dimension of illusion with similar aspects to that of the physical plane. They are able to create any illusion they wish to remind them of their existence in the timeframe from which they just came, or from any other incarnation that they have focused their energy on.

Each time a soul incarnates into form on the physical plane, it brings with it one particle of memory from past incarnations. Upon entering another incarnational experience on Earth the majority of your soul memories are blocked so as to not interfere with your learning experience. A soul will set up prior to incarnation many probable events that it will choose to actualize into experience including the moments that would lead to a probable death of the physical form. Many of the souls of 9-11 were caught in a state of confusion, not knowing that this was the moment of their death as you perceive it. They entered the transition of their energy phase from one focused point of power to another. Since many were unprepared and the event was so sudden, some may linger around for some time trying to communicate with their loved ones. Most however will seek the light of their soul and move on.

Now let me elaborate a little bit here about how manifestation of physical form transcends into the etheric form of energy thus allowing for the transition from third-dimensional reality to the astral levels during a traumatic event.

The victims of any fatal event are prevented from experiencing the great physical trauma of the event. They will be veiled from the physical environment. It is as if they have been encased in a cocoon, removed from their bodies and somewhat set to the side to view the event as if they were watching one of your television sets. In the events of 9-11, these souls were veiled within the last minute prior to the impact of the event. The veiling is necessary, especially in mass events, so as to prevent the souls from experiencing the physical trauma of the event. The same occurred with the victims within the buildings. They were protected from experiencing their reality. Only the empty physical vehicle remains. The souls will vacate the body moments prior to the event. The empty physical vehicle is still able to function to some degree, but without the main consciousness directing it. It is as if one steps into another dimension temporarily and when the time is right, the soul will have an awareness of its present condition and start the process of moving towards the light and on to the Astral Plane of consciousness. Of course in these events there are many guides around to ensure the transition of their energy through the Astral Plane and on to their home Astral dimension. There are many levels of the Astral Planes and a soul's home dimension is predicated on what stage of evolution the soul has evolved to through its incarnational experiences. It is here where the soul will rest and be counseled, as there is oftentimes some level of trauma to the soul. The soul will be showered with an abundance of love and may have to be cocooned for some period of time to rest.

This light will guide you to the home Astral dimension
of your soul where you will experience, through
the use of a hologram, visions familiar to you...

Whatever is comfortable for the soul entity will be manifested by beings from the Astral dimensions to help the transition. All souls when moving out of the Earth dimension will first enter into the Astral plane where they must seek the light and move through it. Many who have had near death experiences describe going through a tunnel. This is the silver cord that is connected to your solar plexus. In the dream state and often when individuals wish to travel within the Astral Plane, they are tethered to their physical vehicles by this cord. When a soul experiences the Earth death process, its energy travels through this silver cord that appears as a tunnel. After passing through the cord, the energy must pass through the Astral Plane and into the light, the light of your soul's essence. This light will guide you to the home Astral dimension of your soul's energy where you will experience, through the use of a hologram, visions familiar to you. There will also be other energy forms commonly referred to as guides waiting to assist you. For those of you whose light does not shine very brightly because of your actions or lack of in the life or lives that you have experienced, this may be more difficult. If you are heavily grounded in the materialistic realms of your world, you may also experience a pulling to go back to Earth. There are many souls wandering around in the Astral Planes trying to find their light. Some of them have been there for what would be centuries in Earth terms. The closer you align yourself in this life to the Divine energies of The Creator, the brighter your light will be and the easier your transition. Often these souls have over-identified with their physical vehicles, ignoring the soul aspects of their consciousness and are now left in a state of limbo so to speak, looking for a place to go. If you persist in identifying with the materialized form of the physical vehicle only, and ignoring the soul aspect of self, it will be harder for you when it comes your time to make the transition. You will find yourself imprisoned in a sea of uncertainty and confusion. The situations that the deceased find themselves in will vary greatly depending on their own life experiences and beliefs.

It is these entities that greet the soul,
but with the physical characteristics that the soul has
in its most recent memories...

Now, as you move on, information from the soul's memories are used to manifest images of their loved ones

6

that have departed the Earth. This holographic matrix is where you will be greeted by the illusion of these relatives that have already made the transition. They will be in the light matrix and the recently departing soul's energy from the Earth plane is to move towards that light. For instance, if your mother or father had already made the transition of their energy, the soul will most likely want to connect with them during their transition. The image of the mother or father will then be manifest through a holographic matrix in a form that is most familiar to the soul that is leaving the Earth plane to allow them to cross through the Astral Plane in a more comfortable fashion. It is these entities that greet the soul, but with the physical characteristics that the soul has in its most recent memories. It is important to remember that most often these are energy guides manifesting images familiar to you. However, if your friends or relatives are not already engaged in other stages of activity, then they will manifest and greet you. I would make another clarification here if I may. I use the word "soul" here as it best identifies with your terms in your reality and it is meant to show you that you are independent from physical form. Your physical form or vehicle is the tool provided to you-the-soul for communication in the third dimension. It is a body and as such has its limitations, and when its life span is completed it will be returned to the energy source from which it came and transformed into something else.

*You can think of it as a theme or contract...so that
you can understand that there was a purpose
for you coming to this planet...*

Souls will often incarnate with the same souls over and over again and the soul will be looking for the most recent version of those souls since it is still tied very much to the Earth plane from which it has just departed. Once the soul has moved into their Astral home dimension, they will then be counseled with their energy guides present and prepared for a life review. This self-examination may take, in Earth terms, many months, or many years. It usually depends on how much trauma the soul experienced, but a life review is always in order. That will take precedence over anything else after the entities have settled into the reality of their energy transition. The life review is necessary and done only with one's spirit guides as you call them. It is a private matter. The other entities that have incarnated with the soul will not be involved in that process. During this review, the soul will then realize whether or not its contract has been fulfilled. (I use contract again as a human term, it is really the choosing of a group of experiences that the soul wished to actualize and whether or not the soul was able do so. You can think of it as a theme or contract, whatever fits into human terms so that you can understand that there was a purpose for you coming to your planet.) On Earth, there are many stages of development of the consciousness and in order to evolve one must complete these stages. Now I am putting this in the <u>most simple</u> of terms, as there is a far greater depth to all of this. I would refer you to some of my other works, i.e. *Seth Speaks* for greater detail.

This contract is between you and The Creator and is a necessary step in your evolution as a soul. You are part of this infinite energy source. You are an extension of this energy and within the framework of your physical vehicle you are experiencing your life with The Creator's energy light source. It would be physically impossible for the energy of All That Is to take on a body of its own because the energy is so massive that it could not manifest all of itself in the limited space of one body, nor would a body be able to withstand it. That is why souls have been created. Each soul is a spark of this vast energy source and all of its experiences are also experienced by All That Is. It is the soul's nature and desire after perfecting itself to eventually merge with this energy source.

After you have taken a rest period for a while and have examined your life, you will then be counseled and you will study and you will learn as you have always done how to manipulate energy. You are the co-creators of your Universe and everything in it. This task is beyond your third-dimensional abilities, however eventually as you evolve you will be creators of planets and life forms. I shall not go into detail about this at this time, since we are dealing primarily with your reality in the present time, as you know it. After your life review and rest period you will be given another opportunity to move forward on your evolutionary path.

A review through some of the many holograms of available experience will help you with those decisions. It is of your choosing however, because as an Earth plane initiate you have free will to move as close as you wish to the energy of The Creator and at your own pace.

That dimension is quite lovely and is meant to be a reminder of Earth but with far more beauty...

Since there is no time outside of the Earth dimension, you may focus as many portions of your energy in whatever life experiences you wish to learn from within the evolutionary framework of your soul. The soul's perception of this will seem to be an eternity, however all will eventually want to move forward and continue their evolution. When you were asking about a television program with the psychic that you viewed recently, that person is communicating with souls who are waiting in their home Astral dimension. They are in transition. They are able to create whatever realities they wish in this transitional period. That dimension is quite lovely and is meant to be a reminder of Earth but with far more beauty. It is a peaceful place where souls may reflect on their lives and commune with one another. Many are quite happy there for long periods of time. This is similar to the heaven that you envision in your religious belief systems, however to be in Heaven is really the merging of your consciousness with the infinite energy source of All That Is.

1. THE CONTRACT OF LIFE

Souls that have committed atrocities against their fellow man are not allowed into this restful Astral dimension. They will be returned to the Earth promptly, reborn to relearn. This return would be similar to your visions of hell because the soul will not be able to experience the peacefulness of its home dimension and once again experience the feeling of separation from the Creator. It would be returned to the negativity of Earth with all of its turmoil. However, the main focus of the soul between transitions is to study and learn from its experiences and move on in its evolution to higher-vibrational planets or go into service with one of the lower-vibrational planets and assist those souls in their evolution.

One must fully transcend all levels of experience in many life forms before evolving to this level. The more life experiences the soul chooses to experience and learn from, the closer it gets in moving into the higher vibration of its evolution. The Christ, Buddha, Krishna, and many more are all members of your planet's Hierarchy and are fully capable of incarnating in self-made bodies and do not have to go through the birth/death process. These entities no longer need to experience a physical life as you know it, for they have transcended the limitations of the third dimension. These entities that have lived many lives on your planet have chosen to remain in Earth-service in this phase of their evolution. Some of these entities have already entered into your world. They have come to assist The World Teacher who has already manifested his body and is gently working among humanity to guide the beings of your planet to your new level of consciousness.

On all planets there are various levels of Hierarchy working with the souls of those planets. They are all in various stages of their evolution. Your planet's Spiritual Hierarchy is presently working to assist humanity in its evolution. These beings are associated with the various levels of spiritual development and religious beliefs of the citizens of your world. Each one is working with their groups at this time to begin the unification of consciousness and realign all of your spiritual and self beliefs into a oneness with Hierarchy and the planetary Creator. Your spiritual ignorance is what has caused so many of your problems in your world. The World Teacher is The Christ himself and this being is highly evolved. He is one of the most evolved beings associated with your planet. All of these beings were once men with physical bodies as you have, they are just further along on their evolutionary path. They are here to teach you at this critical time in your evolution.

You will meet these souls again. In most cases
you have spent many lives incarnating with them...

The Contract and Learning from the Loss

You are on your planet to learn and evolve. When you have finished learning one incarnational group of experiences you will move on to another incarnational group of learning experiences until such time as you have mastered the Earth experience and can free yourself of its limitations. All souls need to move on with their evolution. When you allow your life to be severely affected by the transition of another soul, you do not allow that soul to enjoy the peaceful existence it is now capable of experiencing. The constant longing for the soul to return to the Earth plane by its loved ones can have serious effects on the soul. For then instead of seeking the light and accepting the transition, the soul becomes absorbed with feeling the need to return to an Earth-life existence without the proper amount of rest time needed in its home dimension prior to the next incarnation. Their energy becomes trapped on the Astral Planes, not making it through to their home dimension. Some of these souls, because of the pull from their loved ones still experiencing a life on Earth, will hover in the Astral Planes for many years wanting desperately to return. Try to realize that by holding onto them you are not allowing them to be set free and move on with their soul's evolution. You will meet these souls again. In most cases you have spent many lives incarnating with them. They are part of your soul group that may contain a large number of entities or just a few. You play various roles within the family hierarchies, each time experiencing different elements of life within these structures for the greater learning of soul.

The scripts or contracts that were made by you and the rest of the members of your soul group were set into place long before you incarnated into this life with the understanding that you would each play a role in the learning experiences of each other. Some may play perceived negative roles, others perceived positive roles, but it is all agreed upon for you to learn from the experience.

Now, the souls who have moved on are also moving on with their evolution but the lessons still remain for the Earth souls who are in the process of experiencing their chosen lives. You are to gain a valuable learning experience from this loss, as agreed upon by you before you incarnated into this life. It is your responsibility to continue with your contract until it is completed and you are able to make the transition yourself.

Of course you feel sad at your loss, but it is really not a loss unless you see it that way and this becomes an ego perception. You create your own ideas about how you feel with your thoughts. The impetus behind thoughts is generally ego-motivated in this phase of your evolutionary path. If you choose to be happy then you will be happy. If you choose to be depressed and fearful, then that is what you will get. It does no good to dwell on the loss, for as I said earlier, it is not a loss but a transition from one state of energy existence to another. Allow the departed souls to move on by creating loving thoughts of joy for them that they are able to return home to where you all have come from. As you release them into their new existence, do it with an abundance of love and support. Know that you were not left alone so that you could wallow in your own misery but that you yourself are now entering into a different learning path for your own soul's evolution. The love light of The Creator will surround you and will never abandon you, for you are not separated from it. All you have to do is focus on the Divine energy of The Creator and you will be helped immensely in evolving your soul's experience. All you have to do is ask. You can do this in either prayer or meditation, whatever is comfortable for you within your spiritual belief system.

The rules are very clear about suicide. You may not take your life. It is a violation of Universal Law...

Suicide

I am going to deal with another subject right now, and this is related to suicide with 9-11. It is important to understand that your body is a gift. Some of you may feel the pain of your loss is unbearable. Please know that the souls involved in 9-11 chose to experience this probable death not only for themselves - for their own soul's growth - but for yours. The rules are very clear about suicide. You may not take your life. It is a violation of Universal Law. Some of you may feel you cannot go on. You must stay to finish out your life and learn the lessons that you were brought to the Earth plane to learn.

The suicide mission entities have already been returned to incarnate in the bodies of babies in relatively the same conditions and circumstances. They will be returned into the same mass belief system of the nations from which they came and will have to try again to move towards the light. When a soul sheds its body, if the soul has created death for others or committed suicide, it is not allowed to re-enter its home dimension. The energy guides will escort the soul to Council where the soul entity will be advised by the Elders of the Council to return. A suicide can only be justified on an individual basis with the members of the Council and the soul present. There are only a few situations where it is acceptable. I will further elaborate. If you are terminally ill and your vehicle was in the final stages of the death process you will be allowed to re-enter your home dimension. If you have abused your life with drugs, alcohol or whatever, this is also considered a suicide and you will be returned to do it over again. The Council is the only force on the Astral Planes that makes these decisions when there is a borderline situation. Otherwise, it is fairly clear, you will not be permitted to enter your home dimension.

I may clarify what the home dimension is here. The home dimension of the Astral level is where most souls go to commune with each other and study. There are many home dimensions all based on various stages of evolution completed. As I said before, it is a beautiful place. It is very peaceful and loving and it is where you spend most of your time in-between incarnations on the Earth physical plane. The souls there will make their decisions as to whether they wish to transfer portions of their energy again or not and what planets they choose to go to although most will remain in Earth incarnations until the Earth experiences are completed.

Where you choose to incarnate and in what form is predicated on your spiritual evolution. There are certain experiences that one must master before moving on into the higher dimensions. All beings joyfully choose the type of body they wish to inhabit based on what experiences they wish to have while in that vehicle. Vehicles whether physical or etheric are tailored to the dynamics of the atmospheres in which they reside. Many life forms are simply not perceived by third-dimensional vibrations, therefore you would be unable to see them but they still exist and will be experienced by the soul at some point as part of its evolution.

Effectively it does no good to linger in thoughts of guilt, for essentially there is no such thing anyway...

Guilt

For this next session I want to touch upon the perceived feelings of guilt. Perceived is exactly what they are for they are manifestations of your own mind experience. It is not a good practice to use guilt to blame oneself for the events that cause you to perceive your discomfort. If a choice was made that did not achieve the desired results, then so be it. It was a learning experience and most likely you will have learned from it. Then one moves on. By allowing yourself to feel guilty about a situation, you are again setting up a chain reaction within the framework of your body consciousness to receive more than just guilt. These thoughts express themselves into many forms of illness whether mental or physical. They will begin to manifest because you have taken away the free will of your cells and injected into them your ideas and thoughts, thus changing the healthy and happy path that they were on in creating a whole and healthy being - You. Thoughts of this nature alter the consciousness of your cells, which in turn will affect the ability of your body consciousness to keep your physical vehicle healthy.

Effectively it does no good to linger in thoughts of guilt, for essentially there is no such thing anyway. Guilt is a manufactured production of your own mind/thought energy. Guilt has no purpose. Punishing yourself with guilt only locks the doors on forgiveness of self and shuts out The Creator's light. Realize that by letting go of the feelings of guilt and changing your conscious thoughts, you will have done more good than you are aware of. The thoughts that you harbor, when interplaying in the negative arena, only serve to suppress your own soul's growth.

I know some of you are saying as you read this that it all sounds well and true but how can I make myself stop those ideas from manifesting themselves? Be consciously aware of them. Look at and examine the underlying reasons that you have those thoughts and feelings. Examine the physical sensations within the structure of the thought and analyze it. Are there other feelings and thoughts that have also participated in the creation of these sensations? You will see that there are indeed and perhaps many of them. Much can be said about the nature of your personal thoughts since they make up the nature of your very being. Without them you would not exist. When you can examine your thoughts on an honest level you will see that you have created not only the guilt that we have been speaking about, but also a host of other feelings that in some cases are interfering with your soul's evolution. I will be including several exercises within this book that will help you with analyzing your thoughts and realigning your beliefs.

Your physical vehicle is a marvelous thing, a very wondrous and ingenious invention. It is for your enjoyment, for you to experience all that the Earth plane has to offer. It is not meant to be locked-up in some closet of guilt or hidden under veils of fabric. Now I'm not saying that all of you should run out and strip off all your clothes and run willy-nilly into the streets, because of your society's rules you would probably be arrested. Use this as a metaphor to release your ego's energy from the bondage of its perceived beliefs and open up your powers of creativity. Learn to look at your fellow man with a renewed interest in his being. You are all part of the same Divine energy source. As we observe your behaviors we send much love to you. It is the desire of all essences of the Divine energy of The Creator to live harmoniously with each other. Enough said on this subject of guilt for now. The messages that I have brought forth here can be applied to any situation where a perceived negative emotion surfaces and you have the desire to eliminate it from your perceived reality.

*This event was a wake-up call to humanity
and is one of many that are still to come...*

Negative Energies

All of the souls who made the energy transition in 9-11 knew before coming into this life that they were going to be part of a mass awakening of consciousness on the planet by experiencing that event. Their transition from their Earth existence was worked out long before they were born. These brave souls knew that this event would realign the consciousness of mankind and start the process once again of moving you forward in your stagnant evolution. Their efforts were not in vain. Many of you came into an awareness of self and your relationship with the rest of humanity after this event. Your thoughts and ideas in your present reality are manifesting into actions now that are greatly affecting your future reality. As you move further into this material I will be stressing the importance of your thoughts on your reality and what you can do to change your world for the better.

Oftentimes when mass societies fall upon times of great stress, events will take place to redirect the consciousness

1. THE CONTRACT OF LIFE

The plagues in Egypt were most likely that were a purpose of awaken[?]

back towards a peaceful existence. As with plagues and wars, these events were orchestrated for the evolution of mankind. Many beings must learn from these events in order to maintain an equilibrium that is beneficial to the social order of their societies. The souls of 9-11, prior to incarnating into their lives, were aware that these events were a probable reality and could lead to their probable deaths although they were not consciously aware of it as they lived out their daily lives. All probable reality is based on the actualized thought forms and free will of mankind. There were many, many others that for whatever reasons did not participate in the event, even though it was a probable reality for them as well.

The terrorists as you see them, for they do terrorize humanity with their beliefs, are no different than you or I in their soul's essence. They are still part of The Creator's energy source, however misdirected the ego-perceptive thoughts and actions of their physical vehicles are and have been. We are all connected as one within the many Universes. I realize this is hard for many of you to accept. Anyone who terrorizes individuals or nations is under the influence of negative forces and this should be apparent to most of you what you are witnessing. This event was a wake-up call to humanity and is one of many that are still to come until the leaders of your countries can put down their nuclear weapons and other weapons of mass destruction and start to help the people of the world out of their grip of poverty, fear and suffering.

21

*In this moment of your history you are witnessing
the breakdown of many institutions that you thought
were untouchable and indestructible...*

If you will only stop and look at the information that you hold as true and see that for the most part you have unconsciously and consciously accepted the thoughtforms as being the norm. You have become complacent with the ideas of others and that all of society is evil and out to get you. When individuals are under the influence of the negative ego energies it would appear to be so. This is only an illusion, a temporary situation in which an individual has been caught in the web of these influences. With the realization that these forces exist, one can become more aware and thus begin to keep them from clinging to your light.

In this moment of your history you are witnessing the breakdown of many institutions that you thought were untouchable and indestructible. You are being awakened to the atrocities of your world and in doing so you will be in direct confrontation with many of the darkest forces of your planet. You will see more of this crumbling of your belief systems in the near future. This is part of the process of the evolution of Earth and its citizens. There will be many more breakdowns in society's <u>firmest</u> beliefs, for many of these beliefs do not hold any truths.

All souls have a built in desire to evolve, but because they have allowed outside forces to take over they are not sure how they will accomplish this. Many of you walk around in fear and despair because you have allowed your perception of the events around you to undermine your soul's purpose on your great Earth. I will give you a very simple exercise here to remove negative forces from influencing you. It is important for you to learn how to filter through and remove information that comes to you. Most of you take everything you hear from your leaders and media as truth. These truths that you believe to be truths are not what they appear. You can examine all data that comes into your mind and purge out what does not give you a positive approach to life.

EXERCISE:
THE BOX

When you find yourself fearful and thinking negative thoughts or being bombarded by them through the dialogue of others, when you are unable to break free of the situation, I would ask you to do the following: I should have you create a small box, an imaginary box. You will carry this box with you wherever you go. When besieged with negative information, take the thoughts, open the box, put them in and close the lid. You may envision yourself wearing a small little box around your neck or carrying it in your pocket, but each time you become aware of an onslaught of negativity and you cannot get away from it, put it in the box. Put them in there and consciously remove them from your thoughts. This works quite well with not only thoughts, but people too. You may put the image of a whole person in there to be cleansed and returned whole back into the Universe. Each time you do this, you are helping to clean up the negativity of others even though they are not consciously aware of it. Put them in there with an abundance of love, no matter what they have done to you as you see it. When this is done with love, it will transmute back into love and back to you. Now, if you find the negative thoughts or people coming back into your head or life, simply open the box and put them in again until you get good at this. It will be routine. Now the thoughts may be hatred, greed, prejudice or anything that's coming your way. If you're driving your automobile and you suddenly create a hateful or a negative thought against another, stop yourself, grab the thought and put it into your box. So you see this works both ways, incoming and outgoing.

The thoughts of mankind are neutralized by the higher-dimensional beings as they float into the Universe. We do not allow your negative thoughts to interfere with the lives of other beings in other solar systems. Since thought is energy and energy cannot be destroyed, we have very effective methods of neutralizing your negative energy through the use of crystals and then returning it in the form of love-energy back to your planet. When you put your thoughts of negativity into the box you are doing the same thing that we are doing. Picture the box as a deep well lined with crystals at the bottom that will capture the negative thoughts as they fall in and neutralize them. When putting a person into the box, imagine them being surrounded by the healing energies of the crystals. If you do this often enough, you will begin to notice a positive change in yourselves and others.

CHAPTER 2

The Soul's Evolution - You Are All One

The Soul's Reality | Evolution of Race | Exercise: Speaking
to Strangers | Cultures | Hate & Anger | Moving Forward |
Exercise: Working Through Your Thoughts and Beliefs

*Many souls take on a persona that they are comfortable
with whether it is male or female, dark or light,
it makes no difference...*

The Soul's Reality

All souls when not incarnated work harmoniously towards the evolution of all. There is no such thing as
racial prejudice. When making the transition to your home
dimension, in between lives where a body is not needed,
many souls take on a persona that they are comfortable
with whether it is male or female, dark or light, it makes
no difference. Many will pick from an assortment of looks
and mesh them together as a reminder of certain lives

that they have incarnated into as a fond memory of those lives. Others will take on no special looks at all and simply radiate their love light. On this plane between lives you all recognize each other no matter what the current look is. You are able to change these looks at will and often do so. Your essences are well recognized by all that you know and always acknowledged by others that you do not know in a peaceful and harmonious manner. Your thoughts are read telepathically there. You are just coming into an awareness of this ability while incarnated in this phase of your evolution.

What I am getting at here is that this is the way you should learn to view others that are not of the same race or beliefs as yourself. You are all sprung from the same energy source and you are all connected as brothers in the Universe. It is your decision and yours alone to choose to incarnate into the type of body and belief system you choose, to further your soul's growth and experience every kind of possible existence, whether it be male or female or a variety of skin colors available to you. You have all been members of the same races that you now hold prejudices against. Since you are living all of your lives simultaneously, the thoughts that you have in this life will affect the others. (I will go into greater detail about simultaneous lives later on in this manuscript.) Taking this to heart, it would appear to be that if mankind would get his act together the future would indeed look quite bright.

*Your preoccupation with good and evil has led you
to believe that white is right and dark is bad...*

Evolution of Race

There is a plan and a purpose with regards to the evolution of races. Now I am using the word race here because it is your term and I will stay within the framework of those ideas. What you consider to be races are not races at all, but variations on the same theme, themes that you have created. It was a combination of many factors much in the same way the planet was formed. The physical body types were created by The Creator to survive within the different climatic zones of the planet. That is it. Darker pigments were given to man when he was exposed to higher levels of sun. Lighter pigments were used where the sun shone less frequently. The darker pigments were there to protect the skin. It shouldn't come as any surprise to anyone and if you look at your hemispheres you will see the logic. You don't see a bunch of pasty white people living in South America. That was the intention.

Now, some beings were brought here from other solar systems as well. They were transplanted for the greater diversity of mankind. You did not evolve from the apes or gorillas, as your scholarly teachers would have you believe. Your scientists may find similarities, however that is all they are. The apes, gorillas and even ancient man were also transplanted here from other star systems. The physical bodies that you currently identify with in this solar system have all come from other star systems before being seeded onto Earth. Most of you now come from the Atlantean civilization and are intimately tied to the beings of Sirius. Therefore it will be impossible for your scientists to trace the evolution of mankind until they open their eyes to the other dimensions of your experience.

You have been able to experience your lives, at least most of you, in one race or another, simultaneously learning as you go, one need fulfilling the other, and so on. Your preoccupation with good and evil has led you to believe that white is right and dark is bad. However this is such a distorted view of the real reason behind the different physical characteristics of mankind, that to us viewing these ideas it appears as insanity. As we observe your logic, it is most sad to see how you have distorted the beauty of this creation with your own ideas and fears. Again, taking something of great beauty and turning it into something ugly in your minds. You then are afraid to face the reality that you have manifested with your thoughts. You have let yourself get carried away with your fear of other beings and your fear of good vs. evil. It is time for you to change the thinking that white is good and dark is bad. The same can be said for the dark races. It is time for you to change your thinking that white is evil and dark is good because you are all in this together, growing and evolving as one. Light or dark matters not in the evolution of the soul. It only hinders your soul's evolution when you place these kinds of barriers on it.

2. THE SOUL'S EVOLUTION

Your perceived reality is only a manifestation
of your mind. Your true reality is a manifestation
of God's mind. All else is an illusion...

Because of these distorted ideas, you have essentially locked yourself into little boxes and thrown away the keys. Living in your separate societies, barricading behind your iron gates, fearful that someone of the wrong color might come in and see who you really are, or take some precious part of you away from you. You need only face your fears to end this perceived reality, for it truly does not even exist. Your perceived reality is only a manifestation of your mind. Your true reality is a manifestation of God's mind. All else is an illusion. You have been quite astute at creating for yourself roadblocks to your own evolution. As you begin to expand your awareness you will be able to learn to trust yourself and your own intuition and stop playing into the forces of negativity that wish to keep you locked in your box. It is time to unite as brothers and start living in harmony with each other. Without each other, you would not be, because you are all connected to each other from the same divine energy source.

It is time for you to start realizing the importance of your relationships with each other. Many of you do not like to think that the events of 9-11 were a wake-up call but I urge you to examine your feelings after the event. Did you not for a short while, (short because we see you waning away again) feel a sense of bonding with your fellow man? Did you not feel the love and compassion for others that you have so long ignored? Look into the eyes of a stranger. You may just see yourself. After the events of 9-11, we were seeing mankind take the necessary steps to move forward in the spiritual evolution of his soul. You were caring about each other. You were taking notice of your fellow man and offering bits of your own wisdom and encouragement. Continue to do so. Just because it seems to be in the past, do not forget the revelations that you have experienced from this event. This event is part of your evolution and if you use the experience to grow and change your world, then those who perished will not have given up their lives in vain. You do not have to play into the hands of the terrorists, for in doing so you will be feeding their insatiable appetite for power and control of your world. Realign your energies to create a new and wonderful reality for your world, a world of peace and goodwill towards others. This is not hard to do. It just takes a sincere desire to do so. Below is another exercise designed to help you break down the barriers of fear towards your fellow man.

EXERCISE:
SPEAKING TO STRANGERS

Go out today and speak to a stranger. Do something kind and look into their eyes. You may recognize them, you may not, but remember you are connected. You are both part of the same essence of God's divine energy. Try to speak to someone whom you would normally not even give a thought to. This will be the hard part, to see if you can break through the barriers of prejudice and fear. If you would try to do this on a daily basis, you will see how much joy it brings to your soul and you will then get a tiny glimpse as to what the true nature of your being is all about. You all may wear different packaging but that is only by choice. Just remember, you create your own fears. This exercise, if practiced daily, will enable you to remove those barriers.

Societies are strained to the brink of war
in some cases as they are seemingly being forced
to accept the belief systems and cultures of others...

Cultures

Let us talk about the cultures of your planet, for this seems to be another area of disillusionment for you. When humans created the various cultures on your planet they were delighted in the creations of their consciousness, the creation of various self-identities. Experiencing this creative ability gave them much freedom to express themselves in ways that set them apart from everyone else. Many subscribed to those ideas and thus cultures were born. One sprung from the other and so on, each with its own certain characteristics that were uniquely its own. There was much diversity as different people decided to try variations on other's beliefs as well as inventing their own. It became a territorial expression eventually as humanity migrated to different areas of the planet. They took with them their cultural ideas and added a few of their own, thus setting up entire civilizations that were then subscribing to different belief systems and cultural practices. It is an ever-evolving thing and you see it today in your societies. Many civilizations are now living in and sharing the same territories and the belief systems are changing and expanding. Bits and pieces of each culture will remain, some will be tossed and others saved as humanity moves further in its evolution. It was all designed to be part of your learning experience on your planet, to give you diversity, a variety of experiences from which to choose.

Unfortunately, you also see the conflicts arising all over your planet as these cultures try to meld into each other. There are strong territorial and cultural beliefs that various nations wish to hang onto. Societies are strained to the brink of war in some cases as they are seemingly being forced to accept the belief systems and cultures of others within their territorial domain. The United States, being the melting pot of all nations, has seen its share of racial and cultural wars. It is too soon to tell as to whether this experiment will fail or succeed. It will be determined by the choices you make and whether your enlightenment is swift or slow. It is all part of The Creator's plan. The North American continent was to be an experiment to see if humanity would be able to live together as one. When entering into this experiment, oftentimes one is searching outside oneself for happiness. Happiness does not lie within the borders of another country, it lies within the borders of your mind. When entering into a nation that is comprised of multicultural belief systems, one will be faced with the challenge of learning from the experience of living together as one nation. Now, in the melting pot these cultures are experiencing great difficulties as they perceive themselves to be under attack by others. But as man moves further in his evolution, he will come to realize with the awakening of his soul that he is not under attack by anything other than his own set of perceived beliefs. The only difference is your perceived reality of the experience.

take a look at your anger, analyze it, feel it, express it within your creaturehood and then remove it...

Hate and Anger

In this session let us touch upon hate and anger, as anger is the precursor to hate. With the emergence of the events of 9-11, there are many of you who are in the hate and anger mode against the perpetrators of the event and rightfully so given your current set of beliefs. The mass evil that was planned and executed was indeed a horrible event. As you express your anger, understand where it came from and let it go. By turning it into hate you are then forced to deal with the pent-up energies related to hate. The hate will eventually turn itself on you and leave you with either an illness or some other form of retaliation within your physical and mental framework.

Your being's natural aggression and feelings towards this event should be expressed, but in a way that does not cause harm to others or put you in violation of Universal Law. Anger is a natural expression of your being and should not be shoved away into the recesses of your minds where it can come back and attack you later. Look behind your anger and you will see a cry for help, either from yourself or others. Now while it is OK to hate the actions of others, it is only OK if you understand the feelings and motivations behind that hate and release them after you have analyzed them. I am not suggesting you suppress your emotions, for that in itself is not healthy. But what I am suggesting is, take a look at your anger, analyze it, feel it, express it within your creaturehood and then remove it. Know that the feeling is there, but do not dwell on it, for anger then turns into hate.

Many of you have much to learn about this subject since you seem to dwell on the idea that hatred of individuals is perfectly OK because you have allowed yourselves to feel this way through the manifestation of your perceived fears. You are running from your own fears and illusions. What are illusions? Illusions are the barriers to your knowledge. They create your fears. They are beliefs that are meaningless. They have no truth. Realize your truth, be one with yourself and you will have no fear. Break free of your illusions, change your reality and your mind will not be able to produce fear. You have the power to remove the illusions and stand in the path of love. Out of the ashes of fear will rise up love, your hidden truth. For when you remove the illusions, truth is always found. When you attack others, you only increase both your fears and the other person's fears. If you help others, you release both your fears and the other person's fears. As you face your fears your anger will subside and your hate will not be manifest.

Now you may say, "How am I going to do this, because I have such intense rage over the events of 9-11?" Having intense rage over the events of 9-11 is not going to do anything but further fuel the fires of the negative energies. It is not going to solve the global problem of terrorism. The energy of your hatred would be better off turned into understanding, to create a peaceful loving solution to help the people of the many nations of the world regain their sovereignty and independence and unite you back together as one.

Moving Forward

Look at the larger picture as to why this happened and you will see that there were many global situations that led up to this event. I will be discussing them later in these writings. No one can hurt you personally unless you empower them to do so. Allow yourself to express your own feelings but then move on. If you harbor anger and hate you will in turn set your body up for disease or disaster. If you wish to remain healthy emotionally, physically and mentally, do not allow yourself to rationalize to yourself that these thoughts and feelings are legitimate. Although they have a legitimate place within your being, they are not legitimate with respect to manifesting another set of beliefs with anger and hate. You will only experience the domino effect.

Consciously be aware of what you have thought about your perpetrators, but at the same time understand that this is not a personal issue slated to go against your very nature. It is an event that took place, an event that involved many. Some of you were directly involved and are experiencing a loss with the transition of the energy of your loved ones to their home dimension. However, to harbor the hate and the anger only stifles the growth and the evolution of your soul. If indeed you want to walk through life angry at the world and the perpetrators of this event and others, you will only find yourself culminating these thoughts and events into a mass of frustration. It will only serve to confuse and alienate your being from itself. It is imperative for you to acknowledge what has transpired. If you cannot understand why it happened, do not dwell on the knowledge that you have not yet received an understanding of the events. Carry it forth as a memory to learn from and leave it as a memory.

Many good things will transpire from this event. Even though it does not seem to you that any good can come out of this, you will see humans waking up to the needs of each other. It will happen. I am not suggesting to the perpetrators that they have free rein to perpetrate their evil acts upon mankind. I am not suggesting that at all, for we have dealt and will deal with them separately. They are not free to run amok through society and create havoc on innocent beings who truly are trying to go to the light whether they are aware of it or not. The perpetrators will be put in check. They may try again and again. However we will not let them succeed with destroying your planet. It will not happen. They will be removed. Following is another exercise designed to assist you in evaluating the source of your anger and thus eliminating it.

EXERCISE:
WORKING THROUGH YOUR THOUGHTS
AND BELIEFS

I suggest to you that you examine one of those thoughts that produces your anger. Work the thought backwards and find out what actually transpired within your consciousness to allow the anger to manifest itself. Oftentimes you will find that you were expecting others to live up to your idealized goals. It is important to understand that others are experiencing their lives just as you are living yours. You are not all on the same level in your soul's evolution. Therefore a situation that you may find offensive may appear to another to be the right thing. It is important to acknowledge those experiences without letting them turn into hate, anger and rage. There are many questions you could ask yourselves as to why you have stood firmly in your beliefs, but the object of this lesson is to find out if those thoughts are in alignment with the divine energies of The Creator. Ask yourself if you-the-soul will be able to evolve yourself towards the light with these beliefs. If not, then they should be abandoned and a more positive approach adopted. In breaking down old beliefs and barriers you will be able to receive new energies from the Hierarchy and move forward.

CHAPTER 3

Evolving as a Species

Responsibility for Your Actions | The Danger Zone |
Free Will - Natural Impulses | Your Point of Power - Now
Exercise: Point of Power

Mankind has conveniently sidestepped accountability
for his actions using whatever forum available
to pass the buck...

Responsibility for Your Actions

Life on your planet was intended to offer to mankind an abundance of diversity. It was not intended that individuals would try to stamp out by any means available what they did not understand or did not fit into their own perceived set of ideals. This applies not only to the destruction of other humans but all species that exist on the planet Earth. The different cultures were set in place as a stimulus for creativity for mankind. It was intended from the beginning that Earth would be the planet that would have beings with free will and that there would be much diversity within its cultures. Humanity has used their free will and often destroyed it at the same time.

Because of your own perceived inadequacies you have sought out someone else to blame for your failures. Civilizations are rife with individuals playing the blame game. You and you alone are responsible for your actions. You have consciously made the decisions. Whether they are positive or negative, your thoughts stimulated you into action and what you have acted out upon you must claim as your own. Mankind has conveniently sidestepped accountability for his actions using whatever forum available to pass the buck. You should certainly be able to recognize this observing the actions of your politicians, as they are masters of this game. Every being if they truly examine their life's motivations will find themselves guilty of blaming others for their life's mishaps. You would benefit greatly if you would rise up and admit your failures and move on without endlessly punishing others for your distorted ideas of your reality.

Each being is here, as I have said before, to spiritually evolve. It is my sincerest desire as you read this material that all of you will put down your grievances against each other and consciously start to respect the life that was given to you and to others. You are very fortunate to have been able to incarnate on your beautiful planet Earth. There are millions and millions of beings waiting to come to Earth that have not been able to because your planet is relatively small compared to some of the others. It can only sustain so much life at one time. Humans should be using this opportunity to enjoy and share the lavish benefits of the planet and interact and experience their soul's existence with all the others who have chosen to come here. It is not one of the more evolved planets of the multitude of Universes, however it has a vast amount of learning experience for those who choose to incarnate on it.

Behaviors of greed, violence, hate and war will only suffice to eliminate your being from ever experiencing your planet when it evolves its consciousness. Planets are being prepared to receive those that do not wish to move into the peaceful harmonics. I am told that Pluto is certainly one of those more inhospitable planets with a magnitude of fear that you have never known. Given your limited perception of what I am saying, many of you will deny what you are hearing, but the fact still remains. You will find out when you experience the transition of your energy upon the death of your physical body, that the thoughts you create now will affect your next reality.

No one is justified in the destruction of anyone else's culture or nation. You are seeing examples right now, with the fanatical ideas of rogue governments and terrorists, that if not put in check, humanity will experience the destruction of many nations. You are to experience and learn from each other, not stamp each other out like mosquitoes. When humanity follows leaders that have taken individuals on a path of self-destruction, then they are only furthering their own annihilation. There are no rewards in that for the soul, none whatsoever. Those individuals will be made to experience what they have done to others in their next incarnation, only their experience will be much harder and it may not be on Earth. You have free will. You may move forward in your evolution or you may not, the choice is always yours.

your planet is in danger of experiencing some very serious events unless all of you examine what you have been doing...

The Danger Zone

At this time on your planet there is a great war going on between beings: those that have positive intentions for peace and goodwill for mankind and those that are in pursuit of negative power for the domination of mankind. The scales are weighing in evenly and that is a dangerous situation for your planet. There are many probable realities in play at this time and it is up to the individuals en masse to ensure that the survival of your planet is taken seriously. Your belief systems should be examined carefully and the necessary changes made within those systems if you as a species are to survive.

Most of you still have many incarnations that you would like to experience and learn from whether it be on Earth or elsewhere. The point here is that elsewhere may not be a very nice option. Much of humanity over the last 30 years has started to raise their vibrational hum and move into alignment with the plan of your world and many of you are ready to receive divine knowledge. Knowledge can only be given to you as you evolve, due to the Laws of Noninterference. As you evolve your consciousness the knowledge is released. It is why I do not give specific solutions to problems, because you are here to learn from your experiences and the answers are not to be just handed to you. It is up to you to work out your beliefs on your own and come to terms with your soul's purpose and evolution in your own way. Many mistakes have been made. Also much has been learned.

At this time though, your planet is in danger of experiencing some very serious events unless all of you consciously examine what you have been doing. Your thoughts and actions will greatly affect the survival of your nations and your world. Never before has there been so much conflict in so many areas of your world. Never before has humanity been so close to destroying itself with its weapons of mass destruction. The negative influences that wish to keep you from evolving will use whatever means necessary to accomplish their goals. The forces of light have been diligently pouring their energies onto your planet in an effort to seal off the negative forces in their own dimension. With those energies many situations will appear to be out of control, but rest assured that the walls of dark must crumble down before they can be rebuilt with light.

Free Will - Natural Impulses

Within the many Universes, Earth is a most beautiful planet. It is teeming with all sorts of life that was specifically created to enhance its eco-system and the experiences of its inhabitants. It is a most desirable place to incarnate and experience life. It is also the only planet where there are no boundaries as to what humans can experience. Free will is pervasive on your planet as it was intended to be. Your stories of Adam and Eve were to help mankind understand that free will was the thrust of his existence. Within the framework of those biblical manuscripts the ideas for humanity's behavior were set into place, knowing that with free will there would need to be some boundaries within societies. Nowdays the boundaries are so restrictive that you have almost lost the ability to experience the very essence of your soul , and in feelings of frustration many wars have been fought.

If you would learn to just dominate yourself
and not others, your evolution would
be swiftly forthcoming...

Humanity knows through natural impulses how to experience itself, but because you have been taught to ignore those impulses, you have suppressed the natural creature-hood of your being. If you would allow those impulses their freedom, a whole world of experience would open up to you. You would joyously be able to experience everything that The Creator had intended for you. You have been fighting with others and yourself because you have not been experiencing those impulses. You have thrown them into one of the dark recesses of your mind for fear that they are bad and only fools act impulsively, all the while denying yourself one of the greatest experiences of your creaturehood. Embryos, babies, all living things are impulsively experiencing their existence. Animals do not suppress their impulses. They do whatever comes naturally to them. They do not question their motives for they instinctively know what they need to do to survive. Babies and small children are always using their natural impulses to develop their experiences in life. It is only when they are taught not to trust those impulses that they stop experiencing them.

If you would allow yourself the freedom to experience your soul's journey, much could be learned and there would be no need for wars. If you would learn to just dominate yourself and not others, your evolution would be swiftly forthcoming. I use the word dominate here, because it seems to be a method of yours to conquer and control everything around you. Everything around you is perfectly capable of controlling itself and does not need to have the interference of another to suspend its experience on your planet. Children are a perfect example of experiencing life to its fullest, that is until the peers and parents inject their beliefs into them. If left alone to experience for themselves the wonders of your planet you would see that they are quite capable of learning for themselves and experiencing life. Certainly I am not telling you not to supervise your children and look out for them, but when your influence is so restrictive that your children cannot experience what comes natural to them, then you are shutting down their creative impulses.

Humans have systematically suppressed the natural impulses of the species at a young age, thus spawning another generation of beings who are trapped into the belief systems of the generations before them. The same old indoctrination, drummed into their minds from generation to generation, eliminating any growth or wisdom obtained along the way. You have been systematically injecting your offspring with fear, your own fears, in an attempt to control.

If you are to evolve as a species, you cannot have societies in fear of their existence and afraid to experience their lives. You will end up with the negative forces claiming your planet as their home. These forces feed off of fear and negativity. They have an intrinsic way of filtering into your everyday way of life and your antiquated belief systems. They have had a hold on mankind for too long and as the fanatic, they will use whatever means available to them to subdue your consciousness and enslave you to their negative way of thinking. The members of the Spiritual Hierarchy of your planet and Beings of Light are releasing vast amounts of energy into your world at present to prevent this from happening. But it is all predicated on how you respond with your free will as to in what direction your planet will move.

carrying out those thoughts in your actions
is essentially what is going to save mankind
from its own self-destruction...

Your Point of Power - Now

These messages that I am giving to you are to enable you to know You, to be in touch with the essence of your being: you-the-soul. Because you are presently focused on this life in this time, the changes that you make in this point of power will affect all of your simultaneous lives. You are focusing a greater portion of your energies on this timeframe now, however there are portions of your soul's energies living out those simultaneous lives as well. You are experiencing all of your lessons at once, you are just not aware of it.

When you experience the transition of your energy from this life to your home dimension, you will be given at some point another opportunity to focus a greater portion of your energy on another one or more of the many lives you have set up for experiencing your spiritual evolution. You will enter that life or lives as you have entered this one, in that point in time as you know it. You will focus a greater portion of your energy on those lives. Now, the messages that you send to those life existences from your current point of power will be received and will affect the life experiences of those lives. This is important because your planet's survival depends on your thoughts. Moving your thoughts and beliefs into a peaceful, loving direction and carrying out those thoughts in your actions is essentially what is going to save mankind from its own self-destruction. You are in your point of power now. Now is the time to utilize it to benefit all of your existences, past, present and future. It does not do you any good to pass the buck shall we say and hope that someone else can figure things out for you. At the end of this chapter I will give you an exercise to help you in this point of power.

Since you are in the throes of a planetary evolution, what you focus on now - the ideas and beliefs that you have now- are what is going to assist you. Many of you are very familiar with concepts about how your energies affect the planet and for those of you who are aware of this, you should be able to see that the effects of this are happening all around you. It does no good to dwell in the negative for this is not the time.

As we observe the planet Earth from our dimension, the swirl of energy around her has been quite disturbing. You have experienced many mass events both in nature and with the behavior of your citizens. Earth cannot sustain this kind of energy for much longer. If its citizens do not start to raise their vibrational hums, the planet itself will revolt against mankind with more and more natural disasters. Since your energies create the weather and all of the planetary problems, it would behoove you to start to take a serious look at what you have been doing. If the citizens of the planet surround themselves with an abundance of negativity, that negativity will and does create disturbing weather patterns around the planet. Everything in your eco-system is affected by your mind/ thought energy whether you realize it or not. You can eliminate all of the disturbing weather patterns if you change your thoughts and move into a loving peaceful alignment with each other and the planet. If you could see it from my dimension you would be saddened to see the destruction of what was once a beautiful paradise where all creatures lived in harmony with each other. It is not too late to change.

EXERCISE:
POINT OF POWER

As I have mentioned before in other writings, focusing on your own point of power will allow you to know you: your soul. Take five minutes out of your day to focus on your emotional, spiritual and psychic abilities and nothing else. This is of great benefit and will enable you to bring your physical being in alignment with you-the-soul. Focus on you, your soul and nothing else. Bring to your thoughts a desire for an awareness of your being. Listen to the hum of you, feel the vibrational hum of your being. Again, do this and then forget about it. It's that simple. Notice how you feel after the five minutes are up. For the human vehicle it can be almost intoxicating to suddenly become aware of the soul aspects of self and the peacefulness that surrounds it when the ego is not involved. As you do this daily, you will start to increase your own vibrational hum and move your being into alignment with the planetary evolution.

CHAPTER 4

Moving out of the Darkness
of a World in Turmoil

Corporate Greed & Globalization | Global Collapse |
Aligning Your Energy | Opening Your Minds |
Exercise: Healing the Nation

*There will come a time when the minds of the few
in power will be halted abruptly by the minds of many...*

Corporate Greed & Globalization

It is time to stop competing with each other and start cooperating with one another for the good of all. The fruitless endeavors of your governments to dominate have brought about many of the circumstances that they are trying to prevent. The leaders of many nations have been interfering to various degrees with the sovereignty and cultures of other nations, trying to strip them of their heritage and individuality and manipulating them into the Western way of life. What I am getting at here is that America and some of the other nations of perceived power must not "assume" that their way is the only way. I am not advocating the actions of the terrorists, however I do see a certain amount of interference from your own country and that of others that precipitated these events.

For years the plight of the peoples of impoverished nations has been relatively ignored by the nations of great power. Those leaders have done little to relieve the suffering of the millions. Instead they have tried to westernize them and force them into accepting the invasion of corporate greed. Now, in hindsight they are wondering why this has happened. They need only look at their actions or lack of to find the answers. You cannot rape and pillage the Earth or its inhabitants without suffering dire consequences for those actions. It will not be allowed. There will come a time when the minds of the few in power will be halted abruptly by the minds of many.

The Corporations of the world are forcing their products upon many of the world's citizens...

Corporate greed is rampant within the Western world and the mass globalization of the capitalistic dream has left many countries in fear for their own sovereignty. When two thirds of the world is starving, as it is today, and the rest of the world is ignoring their plight, as it has been doing, terrorism will continue. It is the cancer of your societies today. Many in the so-called civilized nations of power bathe themselves in luxury, spending their money on materialistic goods that have been forcefully produced by undeveloped countries that cannot even afford to grow their own food, because of the demand for products from the Western world. If you will, just observe around you and take notice of how wastefully your fellow countrymen spend their money on frivolous objects of pleasure while at the same time ignoring the plight of millions of starving people worldwide. Because it is not in your own backyard, you refuse to look and see. You refuse to get involved. One cannot justify these situations by saying that this is what the people want, for it is not so. All of mankind should be able to enjoy all of the benefits of life on this planet, not just those who have money and power within their nations. The corporations of the world are forcing their products upon many of the world's citizens, wiping out their way of life and slowly spoon-feeding them a diet of Western greed. It is sad for those of us in my dimension to observe the careless way that the so-called civilized world views the rest of humanity. They are them, apart from you as you see it, but you are all one in the same.

The mass globalization of the Western world into the lives and cultures of other nations fuels the fires of anger of the citizens of those nations. Corporate greed is stripping them of their identities and their power to sustain themselves. While the Western world is busy spending lavishly on themselves and feeding their bank accounts, they look away from the other two thirds of the world struggling to stay alive, two thirds of the world's people who know not where their next meal is coming from or if their children will live through the night. The Western world and some of the other nations of power are busily creating useless objects - trinkets - from the sacrifice of other life forms, and every conceivable gadget to hold the limited attention of those who already have so much yet they are constantly on a mission to obtain more. The few organizations able to help are forced to beg others for money. The "Others" are most often willing to donate only if it serves a corporate purpose i.e. tax relief. There are those who will say that they give, and some of you do, but what are the true motivations behind the giving? When the giving comes sincerely from the heart, then and only then will you be able to see the need of the starving millions and understand the soul's mission. As long as the giving is a political and corporate decision, it is without merit, for it truly is not given from the soul.

What is the ego? It is like a tiny voice offering you everything, but really nothing. It is your creation...

If one would consciously examine their life and their monetary assets it would be acutely obvious that much of what you spend is spent on your desire to make yourselves feel better. All the material possessions in the world will not make you feel better, for you-the-soul knows better. They are but desires of the ego. What is the ego? It is like a tiny voice offering you everything, but really nothing. It is your creation. You have given power to it by believing in it. It will foil any attempt at your knowing the true feeling of feeling good. For feeling good to the soul is watching a starving human being eat a meal that is nutritious and seeing those individuals have proper health care and shelter. Allow the ego to slip away and your true self will emerge.

Global Collapse

The world is on the brink of a global collapse. No longer can mankind blame anyone else for his situation, for mankind has not been willing to help others or to take an interest in anything that is not within the realms of his own isolated illusions. If each one of you readers would look at the world in a different light and begin to help others less fortunate than yourselves and share the wealth and resources of your planet, there would be no need to fear and fight with each other. There is an abundance of resources available to mankind on your planet, yet the few nations with the most power and corporate interests have managed to hoard them all for themselves. Why is it that your governments have warehouses of food stockpiled, oftentimes just rotting away, and others have nothing to eat? How does mankind justify this kind of behavior? There is no such thing as a superpower in the eyes of The Creator. Superpower is manifested by the egos of mankind for the dominance of others. Others do not need to be dominated. Others need for the ones who envision themselves to be the superpowers to share the planet's resources with them and allow them to have the freedoms and benefits that your Western world so lavishly enjoys.

If the very rich in your countries would get off their pedestals and see that they are controlled by their own greed and illusions of power and start to answer the calls to abandon their kingdoms and help humanity, they would experience the true meaning of love. They would begin to know the love of self, for the love of self is not a materialistic love, it is a love that the soul knows. All the material possessions and lavish vacations in the world will not bring you one bit closer to the reality of who you are, it will only increase the distance between you and your soul and delay your evolution.

When you stand by and watch millions starving, it is you who will be starved; starved of the light of The Creator and the divine nature of your soul and your purpose on your planet. If you cannot see the light, the light will remain dim or burn out all together until such time as you begin to seek the light. It would be quite a different existence to be living one's life as a clam or inside of a rock for hundreds or thousands of years. Yet all is possible, and as the light dims, this may be the path chosen.

Aligning Your Energy

*If you do not support the greedy corporations and refuse
to buy their products, you will force them into looking
at the way they do business with the rest of the world...*

The soul-you knows whether or not you are living a life in alignment with The Creator's divine energies or whether you are allowing the ego to rule the roost. The ego will always look for ways to elevate itself on the lack of others. The Western world is so caught up in materialistic trappings that many of you will simply try to ignore what you have just read. However, once you have read it, the soul knows that it cannot be ignored and the ego is fully aware whether consciously or unconsciously of its actions. You will justify the corporate greed as a means to support your families, or whatever pops into your minds. You certainly have to support your families, that is true. However look at it in a different light if you will. Why not dispense with the items that don't really matter and start to concentrate on useful items for the people of the world. Food, clothing, health care, medicines for the most basic needs, clean drinking water for all, sanitation, adequate and sturdy shelter. There are many useful items that mankind has invented that would greatly improve the lives of the starving millions. You can live a much simpler life. You do not need to live with all the trappings of the ego. Many of you crave the simpler life, the life that you once knew when you were young. These are just a few of the things that would help to restore the balance of the resources of the planet. The world is full of talented, educated individuals that could provide the necessary tools for the underprivileged nations of the planet. It is not about what you have in your world or how much wealth you can amass, it is about sharing the resources of the planet, about loving your fellow humans and taking an active interest in their lives so that all may experience the plenitude of gifts your planet has to offer.

If the wealthy nations of the world would learn to live with less and start to focus their energies on helping others, the entire world would remake itself. You do not have to buy into corporate greed and globalization. You have the power to stop the atrocities with your funds, for you are the ones who can make the difference to those in need. If you do not support the greedy corporations and refuse to buy their products, you will force them into looking at the way they do business with the rest of the world, for they are only motivated by money and profits.

Taking one small step at a time, by each and every one of you who feel that you have had no say in the plight of mankind, you will be able to create a peaceful world where all beings are free to live their lives without fear, prejudice or greed. The majority of you are living in splendid conditions with an abundance of items that you do not even need. Why not take those items and donate them to worthwhile causes or start your own and redistribute the proceeds to help feed the world's hungry. It takes a willingness on your part to see the need of your fellow human beings and do something about it. If you sit back and wait for others to do it for you, then your evolution will sit back and wait for you. It's that simple.

Examine your inner self carefully and you will see your actions as well as the actions of your leaders were responsible for this event...

Opening Your Minds

Humanity cannot continue on its disruptive path of negative energy without having to pay a price. Search in your hearts and you will see what I mean. You have all participated at one time or another in hatred, greed, selfishness, and domination. Examine your inner self carefully and you will see that your or your leader's actions or lack of actions precipitated the manifestation of 9-11 and other events. It is not a matter of good vs. evil, for as I have stated before, there is no such thing as good or evil. Now I know again you have trouble with this because of your preconceived ideas that if there is a good there has to be an evil. These are only realities that you have created. These are realities that you have subscribed to because you are not in touch with your soul's purpose within the divine plan of The Creator.

The Beings of Light that are now descending upon the Earth are bringing many new energies that mankind will slowly begin to accept, "energies" meaning ideas and concepts that have long been forgotten. The souls coming into incarnation at this time are the ones who will lead your planet into its new level of consciousness. We are sending our energies to the minds of mankind at this time, pouring an abundance of our love into your souls and stimulating your awakening. The soul's essence will begin to remember. There is a multitude of information available to each and every one of you. As you awaken you will be able to tap into this information. However, you are encouraged to make the effort to open your eyes and dissolve the hatred and racial barriers to your soul's light. We have been gently stimulating you to awaken your consciousness. When I say WE, I am speaking of myself and many other entities like myself, as I am not unto myself alone, as one would want to believe that I am some kind of super being. I am not. I am no different than you. However, in my dimension where I have ceased to don a dense, physical body, all of my abilities and memories are available to me. They are available to you as well, you just have forgotten how to access them. The encumbrances of your bodies and your pre-programmed ideas of what your world is like have stood in your way much of the time. As you evolve, so do I.

We are very concerned about the Earth planet because there has been so much destruction. Mother Earth can no longer continue on this path. Your planet Earth is no longer in balance with the rest of the Universe. It is off balance and if it were not for the intervention of Light Beings from the higher dimensions, your planet would have been destroyed by now because of your actions. You are swirling in mass amounts of radioactive debris that is responsible for most of the new diseases and cancers on your planet. Each time you build a nuclear power plant or set off a nuclear explosion underground, you are killing yourselves. Regardless of what your leaders have told you about its safety, tiny particles are being released into your atmosphere every day. It is of such great magnitude, that if it is not stopped, there will be no more life on your planet. You have not developed instruments sensitive enough to detect this radiation, however I assure you, you are all breathing it every day. This is not part of the divine plan for mankind. There are other forms of energy available to you, all you have to do is implement them. Eventually you will be able to harvest your thoughts with light through the use of energy crystals but that time is not yet upon you. There are energy sources available to mankind that are free and are safe. As you evolve your consciousness towards the light all will be revealed to you, but until then these secrets will not be given to you. Mankind must prove that he is capable of using them fairly and wisely. At this point you are not ready. Your behaviors are too unpredictable.

Your leaders are swathed in military arms
that are capable of turning your planet
into a cosmic pile of debris...

Western world leaders have focused on their military might with such a vengeance that it is becoming the accepted norm to go after the perceived enemy with all sorts of biological and chemical warfare. Your leaders are swathed in military arms that are capable of turning your planet into a cosmic pile of debris, hurling its citizens into the endless abyss of space. The dire spiritual ramifications of such hateful and aggressive behavior are left to swirl about you like a cyclone of debris attaching itself to the very fibers of your existence.

This is not what the founders of your great nation had in mind when they spoke of the right to bear arms. These acts are not God-oriented and do not conform with Universal Law. I have spoken before on this as "a violation." This is a violation. Intentionally projecting hateful thoughts and terrorizing society is a violation. Spinning like a web around the souls of man, these thoughts eventually suffocate your very existence as you know it and leave you in a spiritual abyss, a limbo of sorts, until you seek the light. This kind of thinking only keeps the consciousness of mankind saturated in fear. You may think these weapons are protecting you, however your soul knows better. When one "assumes" this to be their protection that is exactly what one is doing. Your protection lies in the unity of self with the will and plan of The Creator.

This cannot continue much longer if you are to survive as a species. Increasingly disturbing weather patterns have been experienced across your planet. This will likely continue. The Earth is fighting back, manifesting weather patterns that will serve to wash away the destruction of her delicate skin by mankind. The great upheavals of your mountains spew forth the abundance of negativity that has been injected into the body of Mother Earth. The global cleansing has begun as the Earth prepares for the transition into the peaceful harmonics of the fourth dimension and her alignment with the rest of the Universe.

In order to facilitate the healing process on your planet, the energies of its citizens and leaders need to be realigned with the light energies of All That Is. If you wish to make a difference in changing the reality of your world, I will give you another exercise that, if practiced daily, will begin the healing.

EXERCISE:
HEALING THE NATION

If you will, meditate daily on creating peace in your world by focusing your attention on sending healing energies to your leaders that they become aware of the global problems in your world instead of their own isolated illusions. If you would spend at least 20 minutes daily on this, the mass thoughts of all of you would begin to start the healing. You can do this at any time. You do not have to be in deep meditation. Just focus your thoughts during your daily routine for just a few minutes at a time, sending messages. You may do this, for example, in the shower, driving your cars, anywhere

where you do not have to be actively focusing on your daily activities at that given moment. The more you do this, the sooner you will begin to experience healing as a nation and as a world.

CHAPTER 5

The Realignment of Belief Systems
and the Awakening of Humanity

Tolerance of Other's Beliefs | Questioning the Mass Belief
Systems | Exercise: Analyzing Your Mind-Thought Beliefs |
The Beliefs of Your Leaders | Other Planetary Life Forms |
Re-scripting Your Future

I have said this many times,
'You create your own reality'

Tolerance of Other's Beliefs

Let us talk about the tolerance of others beliefs. Many of you are under the perceived belief that you do not like the beliefs of other races, thus again making them more intolerable to you. You have decided that your beliefs are the only right ones and discounted all others that do not fit into your picture of a perfect world within your perceived reality. Since you cannot come to terms with and tolerate any other beliefs outside of your limited perception of reality, you condemn the other beliefs to "your version" of "the wrong way," always maintaining that yours is the right way. There is no right or wrong way in the greater scheme of things. One group will incarnate into a society that has mass beliefs in one direction while another may incarnate into a society with an entirely different set of beliefs. One perceives the other wrong because it does not fit into their mass-conceived system. You are all incarnated in your present physical system of reality for one purpose only and that is to further the evolution of your souls. These perceived ideas are merely obstacles that you have put into place to learn from. The problem is you have not learned much.

It does no good to stay locked in your narrow-minded version of your perceived reality. You are not benefiting anyone, least of all yourselves. When you observe that entire societies have been raised with their own version of a mass belief system, then you are able to understand why it is imperative that you break out of the mold of the masses and analyze those very beliefs and thoughts that brought you to where you are currently in your lives. I have said this many times, "You create your own reality." You are obsessed with the ideas that you are right and everyone else is wrong. There simply is no such thing. It is a creation of your own mind/thought energy, another attempt of the ego to control your reality.

You have been blindly following the ideas of others without questioning them, taking them for granted. You have simply not allowed any thoughts that do not conform with your strict set of perceived beliefs to enter into your world, thus shutting out the beauty of the world itself. Your own fears of the unknown have entrapped your soul's existence into a stagnant lumbering existence. You were not allowed to incarnate into your world to lock yourself away from the rest of humanity, yet with your actions this is precisely what you have done. You have shut out anything and everything that does not conform to your standards of your perceived reality. It has not gained you a thing except a lot of fear, anger and hate for the same souls that, when you are not incarnated into a physical body, you have a tremendous love for. You come to the Earth plane and decide that you do not like the packaging or the lessons and experiences that other souls have come into incarnation to learn, so therefore you must shut them out of your existence. You don't like what you see. You don't want to see. You are afraid to see, so see you shall not. No one is at the mercy of another's beliefs. Each one of you has the free will to change your system of beliefs.

When the ones in power can persuade the masses to believe that killing is justified, then you need to take a good look at the motives behind their beliefs...

Questioning the Mass Belief Systems

Light is information. It is the knowledge that is yours, within you and available to you. As you see the fall of your religious institutions, corporations and mass belief systems, know that this is the beginning of this evolutionary process and that you are part of it. Do not be afraid to question the belief systems that have been in place for so long. For if they do not allow your soul essence to fully experience itself without guilt or fear, then they need to be examined. If you take the time on a daily basis to consciously examine and alter your beliefs, you can reprogram them, thus altering your own existence and experiences. You can move from one set of firm beliefs into a seemingly completely different set of beliefs by simply focusing on them daily. As your ideas and behaviors change so will your perception of the world around you. Then you have effectively enhanced your experiences and begun the spiritual journey in the evolution of your soul by recognizing the power of your own being. The way to a peaceful existence lies within your thoughts and beliefs.

Many of you are starting to realize the power of your being. You are waking up to the very nature of yourselves and claiming your rights to exist on your planet in a peaceful and harmonious way. The negative ego influences of some of the ones in power have been aware of this for some time and thus you see the aggressive actions taken on the part of those individuals to ensure that they keep their old systems of belief intact. They have been aggressively branching out into all nations in one last-ditch effort to ultimately, in their eyes, control the world and prevent the citizens of Earth from evolving away from the old ways and into the new. The only way for humanity to stop this invasion is to start to reject the belief systems of these leaders. Question the validity and motives behind the ideas that are presented by these individuals. As you use your own powers of intuition, you will see that the agenda of these forces is quite self-serving and designed to prevent you from using your own free will to further the evolution of your soul and bring peace and harmony to your planet.

When the ones in power can persuade the masses to believe that killing is justified, then you need to take a good look at the motives behind their beliefs. Universal Law is clear: killing another for whatever reason is a Violation, plain and simple. It is not necessary to rob the life of another to get your perceived point across. It is only your perceived belief and does not reflect the beliefs of others, that is, unless you force it upon them, forcing them into relinquishing their power over their own being. The repression of humanity by those in power is beginning to erode and will no longer be tolerated by the citizens of the planet. Much of the world is in great turmoil because of the actions of powerful political and corporate leaders.

Often the belief systems of many only reflect the visions of a few. Many individuals simply follow the crowd and do not question as to why they are doing so. This is why so many individuals find it so hard to change their perceived reality, for fear of not conforming within the structures of the belief systems of the masses. They are reluctant to be the odd one out. It is safer for them to go along with the masses than stop and think for themselves, for in doing so they would then have to confront their own reality and belief systems. If this were done however, the individuals would open up a vast amount of information to themselves about the nature of their being and move forward in the evolution of their souls. You would then be able to use this knowledge to joyously go about experiencing your life as you were meant to do. I am going to give you an exercise here that you may use to confront the nature of your beliefs. It is an exercise to allow you to break free of the beliefs of others and find your own path to your soul's evolution.

EXERCISE:
ANALYZING YOUR MIND/THOUGHT BELIEFS

Let us look at the word right. What does that conjure up in your minds? Good, wholesome, upstanding, religious etc. All qualities that mankind aspires to have. Then look at the word wrong. What does this conjure up in your minds? Take a good hard look at this. Dark, negative, unsavory, lack of moral ethics etc. I'm sure that you could come up with at least 100 definitions for each word and that is exactly the exercise here. I want you to make two columns on a piece of paper and label the first column positive and the other negative. Here you are to list words that come to mind in your life that you think of as positive or negative. Now look at your list of words that you have organized into two neat columns. As you look at each word, examine your feelings about each one. What kind of thoughts do each of the words represent to you? What or whom do you associate with these words and why? This is the beginning of examining your beliefs, all of them. Notice that when certain words are examined that they also carry with them certain feelings. These feelings are a direct result of your association with the words on your lists. Many will make you happy and many will not. Consciously look at all of them. For instance, if church makes you happy, then further explore what it is about church that makes you happy. Do you love the unity with other humans that are of like mind with you? Most likely you will say yes. Now, what do those like minds have in common? Do they all elevate themselves as having the true right way that humanity should live? Of course, they all agree with your own system of perceived beliefs don't they? Now, look at the other side of the paper and do the same. You will notice that all those things are in direct conflict with your own idea of your perceived reality, are they not? If you will examine where and how and who put these beliefs into your minds you may start to get the correlation. This exercise is a powerful tool in enabling your conscious mind to be more aware of the beliefs and thoughts of others and how they manifest themselves into your own beliefs. It will stimulate your being into recognizing whether or not it is part of your soul's true nature to accept the information or reject it.

*More and more individuals who are truly visionaries
will soon start to replace the ones who have kept
the great nations of the world in the dark...*

The Beliefs of Your Leaders

This discussion involves the belief systems of the nation's leaders. Many of the world's governments are very resistant to any changes. Politicians go into office with high aspirations of manifesting the ideals that they see would and could benefit society only to fall prey to the negative energies that are inherently manipulating the power structures of the system. Their lack of self-discipline and focus on their own power allow them to be sucked into the rituals of business as usual. They soon see that they cannot accomplish their goals without stepping on the toes of the forces that have held the power. They are entrapped into a system of beliefs that is not their own, however to survive they must succumb to the will of the controlling energies. They have little or no regard for the citizens of Earth as they are enveloped in the unlimited power that they now seem to possess.

The mass belief system that has been maintained by your leaders is starting to crumble. The leaders of the Western world have been quite successful at disregarding the cultural traditions of other nations, thus causing much strife within those nations. There is a constant battle between people of other nations to aspire to be westernized and still remain in the traditions and mass beliefs of their cultures.

5. THE REALIGNMENT OF BELIEF SYSTEMS

There is much resentment over the values of the Western world and many people of so called impoverished nations feel helpless in their situation and powerless to do anything about it. The very nature of their frustration is then taken out in an aggressive, negative way to try to regain their own power. There is much anger over the doctrines of Western civilization. Many citizens of other cultures are rooted in the beliefs that the Western world with all its riches is evil. The Western world has been hoarding all the resources of the world for their own personal gain and ignoring the plight of the rest of the world. They know this and this angers them. They do not like it when the core of what they perceive to hate is knocking on their front doors. Their belief system has taught them that it is wrong to have too many material possessions, yet when you look at the leaders of these nations they are swathed in as many material possessions as they can create for themselves. The rest of their nation is bathed in poverty and resentment. The only way they have to regain their power is to lash out at the perceived enemy. Since it is a mass system of beliefs the anger and resentment is then propelled by the masses of those nations. The natural act of aggression of these individuals has been taken into the negative arena. They see no other way of regaining their power other than to lash out at the nations that they perceive have taken it away from them. The beliefs are so strong and there are so many individuals in this situation, you can see that it could create a disaster of mass proportions.

If the frustration continues at the present level there could be a worldwide war ending with the destruction of your planet. The Western world and some of the other nations of power can no longer afford to continue on their paths of domination. All citizens of all nations must be treated as though they are an important part of the world and not shoved under the rug in favor of politics and corporate greed.

It is a shame that the Western world has been able to migrate its influences over much of the planet thus forcing many cultures to either accept these changes or fight for the sovereignty of their nations. Within those societies you have the pent up energies of those who have been forced to relinquish their own power to perceived higher forces and have been downtrodden with enormous amounts of guilt about their very being. They have been repressed to the point of combustion and as mother Earth acts out in her own way against the atrocities against her in the form of natural disasters, so it is that mankind is doing the same. The basic free will of mankind is being challenged at this point in your planet's history like it has never been before.

Most of the Middle East appears to be in for a slow awakening. The energies of Hierarchy are being concentrated on this area at this time to diffuse the situation but it is not an easy task. The people of these nations are entrenched in their religious beliefs, misguided as some of them are. It is a daunting task and will require much energy from the Masters for many years to realign this area of the world. It will be just as hard for them to realign the Western world, for they are the ones who will likely put up the most resistance to sharing the resources of the world. Either way, the world as you know it is in for some positive changes that will affect every living thing on the planet. We have seen that mankind is starting to awaken to these and other injustices perpetrated by the ones in power. More and more individuals who are truly visionaries will soon start to replace the ones who have kept the great nations of the world in the dark. Just as you see the fall of your corporations you will also see radical changes in your government and the media.

the planets Venus and Sirius are filled with the most peaceful, loving beings in the Universe...

Other Planetary Life Forms

I would like to discuss other life forms and how your thoughts affect the entire Universe. Your thoughts of negativity swirl up into the atmosphere and cling to the spatial grids of the Universe. They must be constantly neutralized and sent back to your planet with an abundance of love so that they do not affect other life forms in the Universe. Beings of Light are very sensitive to the energy created by your thoughts and have been surrounding your planet for years neutralizing them. You cannot see them for they are of etheric matter undetectable to the third-dimensional vision. Much of humanity still clings to the ideas and beliefs that the Universe involves them alone. However, this is far from the case. You have closed your minds and erected giant barriers against your soul's evolution and other life forms. You have encased yourselves in a dark cocoon and locked the door, fearful of what may be out there. For you to discover the true nature of your soul, it would benefit you to open your mind to realities other than your own limited perceptions of self. There are many, many inhabited planets in your solar system and others. There are also many types of bodies, not always physical. Some are etheric as is mine. Mankind's body is designed for Earth's three-dimensional residency and is your vehicle for expression and communication. Your etheric body is your soul and it is within the realms of your physical body. It operates your physical body much as you operate a car. There are many other body types available to beings based on their point in evolution and the planets they choose to experience life on. They don't necessarily have to be flesh and blood like you have on Earth.

Many planets that you would deem uninhabitable are teeming with life. I will give you an example: the planets Venus and Sirius are filled with the most peaceful, loving beings in the Universe. It is a place many of us often go to. In your third-dimensional perceived reality, you often have chosen not to acknowledge other life forms due to fear and your limited senses as to what is out there. You cannot see beyond the vision of the third dimension unless you have developed your etheric vision as a few of you have. When your etheric vision is developed you will be aware of a whole new world. That world will be in the fourth dimension and eventually higher and with that you will be able to see and communicate with other Beings of Light. Many of you now are able to receive transmissions telepathically from Beings of Light and acknowledge them while also separating them from your own thoughts. Many of you though would appear to not be able to do this. That is only because you are not willing. Telepathic communication is available to all of you, one must only learn how to use it. This will be the method of communication in your future reality. As you consciously start to align your energies with the will and plan of The Creator, these abilities will open up to you.

The souls that persist in their life-style of pillaging the planet and each other will be left in the lower dimensions until they seek the light...

It is imperative that you live the life that you have chosen on Earth with the utmost of respect and love for your fellow human beings. You cannot make the transition in consciousness without changing your attitudes about each other. Anyone choosing to experience life at this time on planet Earth is learning some very valuable lessons about the effects of negativity. The great majority of the rest of the beings within the multitudes of solar systems do not experience negativity. This experience has been assigned to the inhabitants of Earth at this point in your evolution. Beings of Light carefully monitor how much the influence of negative energies are affecting the planet. If individuals on your planet continue on their present course of destruction they will miss out on your impending evolution and be left behind. These unfortunate souls will be sent back to the third dimension or offered lives in a two-dimensional reality where they will be able to enjoy the fruits of their greed and negative behavior. The souls that persist in their lifestyle of pillaging the planet and each other will be left in the lower dimensions until they seek the light. The rest of mankind is going to evolve with Earth, where all will reside in peace with a greater awareness of the connection of their souls to each other.

If your leaders attempt to use nuclear power for mass destruction, Beings of Light from the higher dimensions will interfere. Permission has been given to do so. Mother Earth will not be allowed to be destroyed by the fanatical behaviors of those who perceive themselves to be in power. Beings of Light are sending their energies to awaken mankind and assist with the transition of their consciousness. It will take a willingness on your part to promote peace in your world and take care of each other. It means using your free will and the energy of your being wisely to create a new reality on your planet. With your powerful thoughts you will be able to manifest this reality for yourselves. Most of you will have no problem doing this. For the stubborn few that insist on creating mass destruction and dominance over their fellow human beings and aligning their energies with the negative influences, the time is now to move towards the light. Some of you have already started to awaken.

Stay awake, for if you close your eyes again you will fall back into your cosmic slumber and be left behind. Each one of you radiates with The Creator's love and if you look for it in every being you encounter you will find it is there. Open your hearts and minds to being more loving and compassionate towards each other because you are all brothers and sisters evolving together. When you help another, you are also helping yourself and both of you will benefit in your evolution. Forget about what people will think about you because it matters not to the soul. Do what you-the-soul knows is right in your relationships with others. The ego will always try to foil any attempts of the soul to circumvent its authority or challenge it by creating doubts or making one feel fearful of reaching out to others for fear of rejection. The only thing that is rejected is the ego and with this understanding one can certainly move away from that arena and let their soul shine through.

The awakening of mankind is happening now.
You are essentially re-scripting your future lives
during this awakening...

Re-scripting Your Future

One of the areas that the ego likes to control is your emotions. Emotions come from the solar plexus area and are astrally grounded. At present in your evolution emotions have come to the boiling point and saturation levels are high as humanity is getting ready to make the transition of consciousness. This is to be expected, as there are many areas of your present reality that will start to break down as your consciousness makes the shift. Right now the third dimension is astrally polarized but as you move from Astral polarization to mental polarization you will start to gain control of the emotions. This stepping up will also begin to change the vibrational rate of the planet and its inhabitants. As the vibrational rate of the planet changes, the energy component of the beings that occupy it will move into a peaceful realm that has not been encountered in thousands of years. As the planet moves through this high energy field it will eventually move even further in its higher-dimensional fields and complete the next phase of its evolution. The awakening of mankind is happening now. You are essentially re-scripting your future lives during this awakening.

The future of humanity holds endless possibilities for peace. As your vibrational hum is raised so is your consciousness thus affecting your future lives. Since you are able to affect your past, present and future with your thoughts and beliefs, what you focus your energies on now will either propel you into your new level of awareness or leave you behind in the lower dimensions of negativity. As more and more of you examine your beliefs and start to awaken to the purpose of your soul's existence, you will naturally gravitate into higher vibrational frequencies. As humanity loses its fears and you begin to love one another, humanity evolves.

As many of you are now awakening, your souls are starting to radiate a brilliant light. As you move your energies into practicing unconditional love for one another, you are by your own thoughts moving the planet into a higher vibrational hum. Many of you are very knowledgeable on the effects of energy and how it can be manipulated. As Beings of Light you are all energy. Humanity has already awakened to the creative abilities of its creaturehood and is now starting to focus on the evolution of its soul. As you start to awaken from the cosmic slumber that you have been in for so long the receptors of your neurocellular system are being charged with electromagnetic energy. Your planet too will be charged and the purification process will begin. The thoughts of many will create a positive radius of energy bathing the planet. The Earth will move into a tranquility unknown to mankind and eventually elevate itself into higher levels of harmonic vibration. It is not impossible to untangle yourselves from your perceived sets of beliefs and move your consciousness in the direction of Divine Light. Using some of the tools that I will provide, this should be an easy task for those of you who truly wish to evolve.

CHAPTER 6

The Misuse of Religion for the Repression of Humanity

Religious Beliefs | Man's God | God is You |
The Manipulation of Spiritual Truths

*Many of these religions have made it mandatory
to deny your own being and its natural
aggression and sexuality...*

Religious Beliefs

Through the ages humans have always been involved with religion. They have always been aware of a God-energy, but oftentimes have distorted it to serve their own purposes and justify their actions and imposed beliefs. You have used it for various objectives and because of its powerful nature it has become a tool for you to control yourself and others. With the illusion of beliefs that only serve to control your desires you have created roadblocks to your soul's evolution. The natural aggressiveness of your crea-turehood has been so repressed that you find yourself unable to control your pent-up energy at times. You have further damned up your being with your obsessive be-liefs about guilt-ridden issues such as your own sexual-ity. You have denied your being the very pleasures of its creaturehood and again found yourselves wallowing in a sea of frustration.

Take for instance the religious beliefs of the world. Many of these religions have made it mandatory to deny your own being and its natural aggression and sexuality, taking the word aggression and turning it into a negative when it is a part of the natural state of every living thing on the planet. Without natural aggression mankind would not have been able to survive, as his own creative abili-ties stem from this. As a flower blooms, it is performing its own natural aggression. This is a natural process of your creaturehood and when used in a positive way can be very beneficial for your soul's evolution. Even nega-tive natural aggression can be a learning experience, for it forces one to confront their emotions.

If you take a society and tell them that they are to deny the forces of their physical being, the energy that would naturally be released has nowhere to go. It then begins to manifest itself in all sorts of repressed emo-tions until the physical being can no longer tolerate it and the self will act out in a highly aggressive nature or will force itself into an illness. Either way, the power of the being is damned up in such a way as to literally blow itself up. I might add that this is what happens when you hear of people who have been thought to spontaneously combust. Although this is a rare event, it can happen. The pent up energy has nowhere to go. The individual is not given an avenue for release in their own perceived belief system. The belief system in many cases was introduced to them through their religious indoctrination.

Religions have been notorious for trying to control the masses with mass systems of guilt-ridden indoctrination. The so-called religious leaders who were involved in writing the various manuscripts, were well aware that in order to tether you to their way of thinking they would have to make you feel guilty and unworthy, thus roping you into their belief systems and ultimately having control over you-the-soul. This gave them much power, but was in direct conflict with the intended messages of the Consciousness of God. You were stripped of your free will and made to feel embarrassed and guilty about your bodies. The body is a vehicle of expression and learning. It is the vessel with which you communicate with one another. When you truly understand this, you will be free to experience your soul's true nature.

You were also told that you were sinners, unworthy, yet created in the likeness and image of your god. What then does this say about your god? If one were to believe that, then one would have to say that your god was unworthy and a sinner, for you were supposedly made in his image. This is not so, yet you have believed this for centuries, not even questioning as to why. The God of the Universe created you out of his love and in The Creator's eyes you are no less than perfect.

The beliefs of some nations have not changed since the inception of these documents and have held firm for thousands of years without much cause for question. With the advent of modern transportation and the abilities of nations to move their citizens from place to place relatively easily, came a new era of information to many cultures. You now have entire civilizations questioning their beliefs, seeing the rest of the world and the way it is developing or not developing and in a sense confronting those issues openly. Many are torn between their society's system of beliefs and their new ideas of the freedoms that they could have. Many of the beliefs of these nations were directly associated with their man-created versions of god.

The ideas of God being a god of good and evil
also came into play as another way for the religious
leaders to control their followers...

Man's God

Let us discuss mankind's perception of God. Down through the centuries man has always known that there was a force behind the creation of the Universe. Whether it was in his limited environment or in his visions of the stars he has always been aware that there was a greater force other than his own being. Many ancient cultures and civilizations were very in-tune with this force. As highly aware citizens of the planet they had much respect for the energies responsible for creation. It wasn't until the last several thousand years that the power and image of the Divine Creator was brought into a human perception. Mankind felt it was to his advantage to put a face on The Creator, thus humanizing him to however he perceived. Along with this idea the hierarchy of religious leaders decided to take the power of this newly created human god into their own hands. This perpetuated many myths and misrepresentations of who and what God was. The ideas of God being a god of good and evil also came into play as another way for the religious leaders to control their followers by putting their ideas under the name of God. There were many offshoots of the same idea of God and god's, rules and regulations, that mankind was supposed to live by. They lost sight of the fact that God is a force of pure energy that radiates with an abundance of love's light and embodies every living thing. Because of the controlling religious idealists, all power that was once known by all of humanity as part of its own divinity was removed. It was given to this self-created man's god.

You have many versions of God in your nations at this time, all with their different mass belief systems. The writers of the manuscripts that you hold to be true, have had a hand at distorting the original messages at one point or the other and realigning them to fit into their own perceived way of thinking. All of these versions have their various sets of man-made rules, all meant to in some way or another prevent mankind from realizing the true purpose of his soul.

When you remove your judgment, you empower your wisdom. When you have wisdom, you will have peace...

Mankind has been locked in an abyss, waiting patiently, believing that eventually he would be released and able to experience his whole being. His beliefs within the power structures of the religious organizations have kept him in the dark for many thousands of years. You cannot turn the infinite energy source of All That Is into a human. As much as your religious organizations would have you believe it, this is simply not the case. This energy source does not wear one face. It is the embodiment of all living things in the Universes. It is everything in all of creation. All That Is is exactly that - <u>All That Is.</u>

Understand, the leaders of your religious organizations for the most part had good intentions when putting this system of beliefs together, but at the same time, they were denying humanity the ability to experience itself. Most if not all of your wars have been created because of the misconceptions about God, as you perceive him, again "him" being loosely used here as this is your frame of reference not mine. You have judged everyone and everything to the distorted ideas of your illusions. You have been pitted against each other for what seems to be eons, competing and judging rather than cooperating with each other. Until mankind can break itself free from the spiritual ignorance of these beliefs, many more wars will be perpetrated. The belief systems of the masses are able to, so shall we say, swing with the tides, however it will take a powerful force to set things in motion. That powerful force is already manifest in your world as The Christ essence and will soon make himself known to all. Energy personalities such as myself are preparing you for the impending shift in consciousness and the emergence of the World Teacher. Return yourselves to the love that you-the-soul have always known. The soul does not know hate, greed, judgment, evil. These are all things that mankind and his ego self have subscribed to and in doing so, he has fallen further away from knowing the divine purpose of his soul. When you remove your judgment, you empower your wisdom. When you have wisdom, you will have peace.

God did not just sit by and create one planet to be inhabited by one species of humans and then say, 'Well that's it I'm done. I'll learn everything from this group'

God is You

You have always known that you were not in this Universe alone for it is written in your ancient manuscripts and it is part of your soul's knowledge. Through religious beliefs, much of humanity has been locked into believing that they are the only living beings in creation. This idea is so wildly absurd that we cannot help but be mystified as to how mankind has been able to elevate itself in such a manner as to think that the entire cosmic Universe revolved around his limited and narrow visions. God did not just sit by and create one planet to be inhabited by one species of humans and then say, "Well that's it I'm done. I'll learn everything from this group." God, The Creator or whatever term you wish to use, is all part of the same energy source of All That Is and you are part of it. <u>God is You</u>. All That Is encompasses many life forms in many Universes and on many planets. Most of them are far more evolved than Earth and its inhabitants. There are hierarchies and Creator Gods in all of them and in you and every living thing ever created, whether it's a plant, animal, insect or mineral. Everything in the multitude of creation stems from the infinite energy source of All That Is. The Christ Essence is one of the higher members of the Hierarchy of your planet and has decided to remain in service to Earth. This entity could have moved on to other planets and solar systems but chose not to. There are various levels of Hierarchy on all planets in creation. The Christ has been in your world several times to help humanity in its evolution, each time bringing forth messages that would assist in your evolution. Until you can break free and understand that you all have subscribed to the mass belief system of others, and have ignored the original messages of The Christ essence, you have stifled your soul's growth. These messages go back farther than the inception of the world manuscripts known as your bible. But let us look at the bible for instance, for that is part of your Christian world's belief system. Many of the messages from The Christ essence were either left out or distorted and many man-made beliefs and messages attached to it. Many of the messages were so simple but humanity proceeded to distort them to fit into their reality at the time. I will give you an example here: Let us take the anticipated Antichrist awaited by Christianity. According to these beliefs, millions are awaiting the appearance of an Antichrist that will deceive and try to capture them into a false spiritual abyss. This is an obvious distortion of the Antichrist event that has already happened in your history. It happened with the Hitler regime and the slaughter of millions of people on your planet. Millions of people were branded with the tattoo of this Antichrist and thus this prophecy has already been fulfilled. Yet The Christian religious organizations cling to their ideas that this event is still to come. It has passed and as I have stated earlier, The Christ entity is now manifest in your world today and is working quietly among you until such time as he chooses to reveal himself to humanity.

Religions have always to some extent followed the development of mankind's consciousness...

The Manipulation of Spiritual Truths

There are many distortions in other religious manuscripts as well. Much of the information was put into human comprehension with its own devices to control the masses inserted, hence the guilt and repression. The soul was not allowed to joyously experience its being. The nature of the soul's human existence was under speculation and scrutiny. You were given many behavioral modifications because of the perceived fears of the ones in control. Your energies were then locked away from you for fear that if you did not, meaning mankind, succumb to the will of the religious leaders, you would be forever burned in your fiery pits of hell etc. etc. etc. All religions have their own facets of gloom and doom, taking the love away from God and putting fear there instead.

The religious leaders were quite good at manipulating the masses since the masses were under the belief they were not in control of their own spiritual nature. In the beginning there were heavy prices to pay for not staying within the guidelines of what the religious leaders considered acceptable behavior or the norm. No one wished to be burned at the stake. Anyone with any awareness of their soul's true purpose was given the title of "demonic" or "possessed." Nothing could have been further from the truth. They had an awareness that was feared by the religious leaders, for if the masses were aware that the manuscripts that they held to be completely true had been doctored in order to control them and keep the money flowing into religious leader's pockets, they would not keep coming and believing. It was imperative that they be silenced and accused of being witches or possessed by the devil, another way to keep mankind in the dark by feeding him a steady diet of fear, fear of the devil, and in doing so they gave power to the source they had created. In acknowledging this kind of thinking and accepting it into your belief system, you create a reality for it. It becomes manifest within your thoughts and belief systems.

For the most part, your biblical manuscripts were trying to allude you to the fact that your behaviors would affect the outcome of your lives. It was put into a storybook fashion so as to be understood and accepted by all. Religions have always to some extent followed the development of mankind's consciousness. However, not all the written information gives one the truth, since much of it has been distorted and rewritten over and over again. Much of it was deliberately distorted, for the original manuscripts have yet to be found. Most of them are buried deep within the mountains of your planet. The negative influences have also quite cleverly written their own distorted versions of the truth and many religious organizations are following and believing those distorted manuscripts and holding them with much reverence and sacredness. There are and always have been negative influences that have fought to keep the citizens of Earth in the dark about their soul's true purpose.

Now don't misunderstand me here, because there have been many good things to come out of religious organizations and humanity needs to acknowledge their religious beliefs and socialize within the structures of organized religion. It is part of your spiritual evolution as a soul. Many religious organizations are involved in helping humanity throughout the world. They are encouraged to continue and cooperate with the rest of humanity in bringing your world into the next phase of its evolution. It is imperative that humanity's religious forces join together, united as one, for the spiritual enlightenment of all citizens on the planet. Instead of competing with each other, join together as one, and move into the peaceful harmonics of the new world awareness. If you are in alignment with the will and plan of The Creator, then you will recognize when the belief systems of the divided religious organizations of the world need healing. Your energies, thoughts and beliefs are the tools needed for this healing

You would benefit greatly to move yourself beyond the old ideas of one self, one world, one Universe, for this is surely not the case, and in doing so you will experience the vast richness of your being that you have denied for so long. It is important for the survival of the species to open itself up to other probabilities and realities. Questioning honestly the underlying motives of some of the doctrines and rules of the religious organizations will enable you to see that what was supposed to be a joyous positive experience for the evolution of your soul has been doctored to such a degree that it has done just the opposite. It has kept you in the prisons of guilt and repression, thus denying your own personhood.

You have the power to unite humanity and change your world for the better with your thoughts, beliefs and actions. You are the directors of your world and Universe. All comes from you and is within you. God's creation in your world is unending. What he has not created is not real it is only an illusion. You are the co-creators of your Universe. You are all one. You are all Gods.

CHAPTER 7

Changing the Consciousness of Mankind

You the Creator | Communicating with Others | Thought
Health & Evolution of DNA | Exercise: Opening the
Chakras | Spiritual Knowledge

*As your consciousness evolves, you will become a more
conscious co-creator and be able to tap into the vast
realms of knowledge available to you...*

You the Creator

The probabilities now are present for you to quite literally propel yourselves into the harmonics of the higher dimensions by changing your individual and mass consciousness. A vast multidimensional experience awaits all of humanity. Mankind is starting to acknowledge that his consciousness is now beginning to become aware of its greater self. In allowing that expansion there lies the potential to experience the greater realities of your being. It is time for you to take off the blindfolds and open yourself up to the full dimensions of your spiritual, physical and mental abilities. Opening up your consciousness to the impulses and messages that are inherently yours would allow your consciousness to fully experience itself. As your consciousness develops, your neurological and biological systems will evolve. Humans at this time are expanding their neurological connections within the brain. Latent areas often thought of as gray matter with no functional capabilities are being triggered into activity. As this happens your being will become more and more aware of the multidimensional nature of its existence.

As your consciousness evolves, so does your God image. It will move itself towards your idealized goals and probabilities, serving as psychic stimuli to effect change. You are creators of your reality. Your soul-you had a hand in the creation of this planet and all of its living forms. Your ability to manipulate energy and create life forms is second nature to you when you are not focused in this physical Earth reality. Your abilities far exceed what you are able to perceive in the limited third dimension. As your consciousness evolves, you will become a more conscious co-creator and be able to tap into the vast realms of knowledge available to you. Mankind has an innate comprehension of past, present and future probabilities and a built in desire to cooperate with all living species for the greater good of the planet. You have consciously blocked much of this information from your being because of your dogmatic perceived sets of beliefs and your unwillingness to look inside yourself for answers.

Always your ideas of good and evil stand in the way of your soul's development. There are many forces within the world as you know it that are invisible to you. Yet if they were presented to you, you would run and hide, for they do not fit into your limited sets of beliefs. You have been so indoctrinated with the beliefs of others that you have literally dammed up the evolution of your being. From where I am, you would dismiss my energy as ghostly or a figment of your imagination. However here I sit writing to you acknowledging my existence and some of you will still run and hide. You cannot see the wind for example, but you know it is there. You cannot see God for example, but you know he is there, because these are your beliefs. Then why not believe that there is more to your being than your ego-perceptive materialized form. In changing your consciousness, one must acknowledge that there is more to life than what is right in front of your eyes. The total sum of the energy of self reaches far beyond the comprehension of even your most astute scientists. It is there, it is real, it is all of you and it is All That Is.

telepathic communications with beings
in other dimensions will be commonplace...

Communicating with Others

There are many energy entities around you although you cannot perceive them. Since they do not fit into the order of your perceived reality, you deny their existence. You have

been subtley told about them in various sci-fi movie creations although you always portray other planetary beings
as evil and scary and out to take over your bodies. I would
assure you that in this point in time in your world's history
that is not the case. Beings of Light have no use for a dense
physical body on the Earth plane. They have already moved
through that phase of their evolution. All beings are in various stages of evolution and are all part of the same energy
source that is infinite. It would also behoove mankind to
abandon the idea that his death is final. Energy cannot die.
You do not die. Your energy is merely transformed, as mine
is, into another dimension.

It should be apparent to most of you with the introduction of some of your current movies and television shows,
that what you have denied as real, is certainly very real. It is
totally within the realms of your magnificent being to communicate with any or all departed loved ones. It is simply a
matter of listening and not dismissing what you hear as your
own babbling. Those of us who have made the transition of
our energy to the higher dimensions, as well as those who
are still waiting on the Astral levels, are very capable of
communicating with you and you with us. As your consciousness expands, as it is presently doing, telepathic communications with beings in other dimensions will be commonplace. If you would just listen, you would be amazed at
what you might hear. Your conscious lives are so full of
your present daily activities that you have not stopped to
smell the roses, to coin a phrase that you use. Many of your

departed loved ones are anxiously awaiting communications with you. All you have to do is tune in. Their energy is as real as yours and they are no more dead than you are right now as you read this book. They love you and are watching out for you.

Beings of Light are very concerned with the entities on Earth, for your thoughts and actions in your present point of power affect the future of the planet. You have the capabilities of communicating with other selves to influence the life that you are living in different timeframes in order to improve or avoid disasters in those chosen lives. You do this in the dream state on a regular basis. Some of you are now developing this ability in the waking state and are able to communicate with different portions of your energy in different lives and timeframes. That is happening for many of you now in your world.

Just as I am part of both my first subject's and Cas' energy and have been communicating with them, you also communicate with other aspects of yourselves. Both of these entities are communicating with various aspects of the Seth entity of which I am a part, for I am an aspect of their selves in another dimensional-timeframe and they are aspects of my self in their dimensional-timeframe. My first subject communicated with a different portion of my self in a different timeframe than the portion of myself that Cas communicates with, but both are of the same entity-self. Those two lives are portions of my energy, but they are also their own energy, for I am their selves in another dimensional-timeframe and they are my selves in their dimensional-timeframes and we are as one. It is not to diminish either one, as they are both only portions of the total energy that makes up the energy known as Seth, who I am and we are. To further clarify for you, the Seth who I am is also a part of another vaster entity as a whole. So I am only another portion of our total Self. My first subject and Cas both focused on their point of power simultaneously, however my earlier subject has made the transition of his energy into a higher dimension and Cas' energy is still focused in your present reality. We are all part of the same entity only in different dimensions and elements of time and space.

Every thought that you have that has been acted on, manifests itself into one of the probable realties within this life that you are currently focusing on...

Thought Health and the Evolution of DNA

I would like to discuss your thoughts in relation to your health in the present awakening. In order to raise the consciousness of mankind, man himself must be aware of the human condition and the environmental changes going on around him. He can no longer be oblivious to current situations within his own ecosystem and his body. As I have mentioned before in previous manuscripts, you are fully capable of creating a harmonious state of health for yourselves and your planet by virtue of your thoughts. For those of you who are not familiar with this concept I will briefly explain and then refer the reader to some of my previous works for further clarification. Your thoughts create your very existence as you know it. You form your reality based on those thoughts. Your perception of the reality of your thoughts lies within your mind. Thoughts manifest into desires and then into actions. Every thought that you have that has been acted on, manifests itself into one of the probable realties within this life that you are currently focusing on.

Your thoughts are responsible for your state of health. Initiating thoughts that you are sick or will be sick will then set your biological system to receive the perceived illness. If you are told over and over again that you need certain drugs to make you feel better and you believe this, then you are not allowing your own built in mechanisms that monitor your state of being to do their jobs. By believing this, the message is sent that you would rather give the power to someone or something else. You have then set up the atoms within your body to prepare for the invader. Your body is fully capable of healing itself. It is your own thoughts that interfere with the process by sending messages that interrupt the natural flow of things. The atoms of your being are joyously going about their business of creating a harmonious existence within your physical framework and with this thought process that you have engaged in, you essentially throw them a curve. They are now put into defensive mode and must prepare for the attack. The drug companies in your culture are at this time going out of their way to ensure that you are going to be tethered to their product with their psychological messages on your television sets and media advertisements. This very process is harmful to your evolution as a soul.

With the evolution of mankind the current double helix DNA will start to change and move to 12 strands...

As the perpetrators of negativity that have been so cleverly keeping you in the dark for so long realize that the mass consciousness is starting to change, that souls are beginning to move into the light, they are terrified that they will no longer be able to keep you chained to the old system of beliefs. Negativity feeds off of negativity. What better way to do this than to drug the minds and bodies of mankind. Systematically feeding you ideas through your media that you are sick and need drugs to maintain a state of well-being. You then subscribe to these beliefs and send your body mechanisms into a state of confusion thus rendering your being useless in its quest for its own health and evolution. Your body and mind cannot function as they need to for spiritual evolution if they are in a constant state of chemical alteration. The chemical reactions needed to allow your chakras to open to the information cannot take place if you are in a drug-induced state.

With the evolution of humanity the current double helix DNA will start to change and move to twelve strands. Each time it evolves it will do so in a group of three until there are twelve. The evolution of your DNA from the double helix into the twelve strands will correspond to twelve chakras. There are presently seven chakras within your etheric and physical body. During the evolution of the DNA another five will be added outside the body. Those additional five will be the link to the next phase of your spiritual evolution. Much of the information that will be given to you for your evolution will come via these outside chakras and enter the pituitary gland where it will then be transferred into the strands of your evolving DNA. As these new strands of DNA and areas of the brain are activated, brain mappings will be possible and past-life memories will be evoked. Your entire civilization will be based upon a psychic framework rather than a physical one. It is a natural process that every physical being goes through when evolving.

Most of you who experience this evolution will become quite aware of the feeling that you are much clearer about life and seem to know things that you previously weren't aware of. Information will start coming to you in dreams and in states of relaxation, universal information about your being, who you are and what your purpose is and so on. Your consciousness is being raised. The fact that you are reading this material shows that you are searching for the answers and you are evolving.

I will give you an exercise that will help you get started on your own personal path to recovery and your soul's evolution, for you are a soul with a body, not a body with a soul, remember that. Your physical existence is only a temporary one in which you-the-soul are physically incarnated on your planet to learn from your experiences and evolve. Consider it like going to school, Earth school, where the lessons are sometimes harder than on other planets but the amount of spiritual growth that one gains from incarnating here is much greater than it is on some of the other planets and solar systems available to you. If you will take the time to do this exercise once a day and stay focused, you will start the process of aligning you-the-soul with your body as one.

EXERCISE:
OPENING THE CHAKRAS

Sit or lie down and relax your entire body starting from the top of your head to your toes. Breathe deep. Inhale positive energy. Exhale all negative energy and thoughts. Do this as slowly as you wish. The idea is to achieve the level of relaxation that will bring you to a place of being completely free of your body. As you begin to relax, feel all of the tensions fade away into the air as you take yourself deeper and deeper into this relaxed state. Just let all thoughts and negativity float away. You may use the box technique that I gave you earlier to get rid of unwanted thoughts and feelings. Visualize them going into the box or it can be any receptacle of your choice as long as it has a lid on it. Focus on your mental center. For most of you it will be somewhere just above or between your eyebrows, not the area of the pineal gland or the third eye, but just below. This is your mental vortex. Stay in this relaxed focused state for at least a half an hour. What you are doing by this exercise is learning to calm your thoughts and your body so that the Divine information may then start to flow into you through the pituitary gland thus opening up the chakras in that area. As you do this for a while you will start to raise your vibrations to a higher level and you will notice that your difficulties will start to ease as Divine knowledge is placed deep within your hearts. Some of you will be able to achieve results almost immediately while others may take longer. Do not despair as all of you will eventually open up the chakras to receive Divine information at the cellular and DNA levels.

If you feel that you do not want to hear you will not,
but once you have obtained the light there is no turning
back, for you now possess the knowledge...

Spiritual Knowledge

In reading this material there will be many of you who will simply not want to hear. You will go about your old superstitious ways and cling to your familiar and comfortable belief systems. Fear of the unknown will keep you in the grips of the old ways. Light is information. Light is knowledge. If you feel that you do not want to hear you will not, but once you have obtained the light there is no turning back, for you now possess the knowledge. Some of you will want to stay with the negative influences because you will not want to give up your habits and materialistic desires. Whether or not you choose to accept or deny the information that is being given to you is predicated on your own free will. However, those of you who wish to evolve will do so. The rest of you will simply stay in a third dimensional reality with all of its negativity until you make the conscious decision to seek the light. The negative energies, as I mentioned previously, have spent eons trying to keep the light from humanity, controlling the consciousness of mankind for their own selfish purposes. Without negativity you cannot *have* negativity. The negative influences wished to keep Earth as its breeding ground for its source of energy. They are now out-numbered by Beings of Light on the planet and will soon be relinquished to their own dimension. These forces are part of the balance system of the planet, however they have been spiraling out of control for the last several thousand years. Their function was to balance the matter aspect of the planet. They became too powerful though and have overtaken the minds of much of mankind in the materialistic sense and thrown him off course in his evolution. Millions of the citizens of your planet are now deeply entrenched in materialistic possessions and will even go so far as to die for those possessions. This is absurd from a spiritual point of view as these things are only an illusion of your own mind/thought energy and mean nothing to the soul. The only thing that matters is your relationships with each other and whether or not you act on your thoughts and newfound knowledge to help all of humanity. You have been in your dense physical bodies for thousands of incarnations and it is now time to move on to your etheric bodies and interact with each other on a deeper level. Many individuals are now seeing that their evolution is not a physical but a spiritual, soul evolution and are moving towards the light. They are in the process of starting to reject the old controlling theories about the nature of their being and their evolution. They are beginning to realize that they have been controlled by their materialistic ego desires instead of their spiritual desires.

Corporate and political dominators have been the ruling negative forces in your world...

Whole nations are beginning to awaken to their greater reality and purpose in the Divine plan that The Creator has for your planet and are rebelling against the invasion of the old negative influences masquerading in the name of their gods. Corporate and political dominators have been the ruling negative forces in your world. The citizens and believers have been deceptively confused. They no longer know what to believe or whom to believe. They have been told one thing and witnessed another. The art of deception has been masterfully played by these materialistic forces. As you witness many nations and their citizens rise up and fight back, it is imperative not to compete with one another but to unite together by cooperating as brothers in humanity. It is not imperative to kill however. I wish to make that very clear: Killing is a violation of Universal Law. There are other ways to bring the consciousness of humanity into the light of its soul's existence.

There are many energy forces that are free to come and go throughout your world. They usually reside within the Astral levels of your planet. Their access is through the various vortexes throughout the world. The vortex around the Middle East has been an access point for the forces of dark. This is where the network of the perpetrators of your terrorist acts have hidden deep underground and within the recesses of the mountains in their bases of operation. Many of them are nearly impossible to find. Some of these manipulating energies straddle between dimensions in many cases and they are not accessible to the limited perception of the third dimension. However, many of these forces are still there. This is the last stronghold of these forces. They are losing momentum and energy and that will continue.

Nations of the world would benefit by joining forces to peacefully eradicate the restructuring of the belief systems of many cultures to the ways of the negative influences. With the emergence of new positive energies and utilization of the technology of the media, this can be done. Now some of the leaders of your nations of power are very deeply entrenched in the influences of the forces of dark and are going to have to abandon their old ways as well. These leaders will put up the most resistance for they are the ones who will perceive themselves as having the most to lose. They are so deeply entrenched in the materialistic world of power that this will be a great struggle for them to have to make do with less. However with the cooperation of all nations there will be peace for all. You cannot have peace until you have justice in your world. You cannot have justice unless you are willing to share the resources of the planet and care for all other nations and to stop the atrocities of a global corporate takeover of the planet and its resources. This is just a simplistic view of some of the demographics as to how and why 9-11 and some other terrorist attacks have been able to find their way into your societies.

CHAPTER 8

The Realities of a Distorted World

Surrendering Your Power | The Cult's Inception | Exercise:
Ray of Light | Idealists & Fanatics | One of the Leaders

In their attempt to project their beliefs
on the rest of the world, they have attracted
the powerless ones as followers...

Surrendering Your Power

Now, I want to discuss the mentality and belief system behind the terrorists and their followers. Whenever a society has allowed their beliefs to be predicated on the beliefs of one individual it is a recipe for disaster. Under conditions of hopelessness and despair it is easy for many individuals to look for hope in the promises of others. Many individuals are fearful of experiencing themselves and feel that they have no power over their own being. They suffer from extreme feelings of guilt and unrest. Often they become so paranoid and delusional that their reality seems only marginal at best. When the mass beliefs systems of many appear to be the norm, these individuals subscribe to the reality of their leaders instead. They have essentially given up on their own power and handed it over to their leader. Oftentimes, as is the case with the 9-11 event, the leaders are masquerading under the guise of religion. The religious indoctrination in the Eastern cultures starts at a very young age and is accepted by all. Many atrocities have been perpetrated under the auspices of religion.

The leaders themselves are often quite paranoid and their reality straddles between the dream state and the physical waking state. It is often difficult for them to decipher between the two. They are usually individuals with a sense of grandeur and cannot relate to the rest of society. It is their greatest satisfaction to remake their reality into one in which they are the leaders. They will go to whatever lengths they have to at the expense of others if needed to get their point across, all the while feeling completely justified in doing so. In their attempt to project their beliefs on the rest of the world, they have attracted the powerless ones as followers. The reality of the leaders then becomes the reality of the followers all sharing the same distorted set of beliefs. The paranoid leaders then systematically undertake the process of eliminating everything that does not conform to their beliefs. The leaders then often turn into raging fanatics. Since they have now gained a certain amount of momentum it becomes easier for them to reinforce their delusional beliefs. Their followers all along are reinforcing these beliefs. They are indeed frightened of the nature of their existence. They will go along with whatever their leaders have in store for them since they are under the belief that they cannot exist on their own. They are caught between different conflicting sets of beliefs and have decided that they must turn over the responsibility for their state of being to someone else. They are looking for anyone they can to take over the job of making decisions for them.

It is easy to see how the fanatic leaders can gain such momentum. Usually the "evil ones" are perceived as the ones who will not conform to the fanatic leader's system of beliefs. In order to rid the world of these disruptive individuals, in their minds, they must resort to violence and mass deaths, again using religion as the justification behind the cause. I will say this again, "Killing of any kind is a violation of Universal Law." It is not tolerated and when these souls make the transition of their energy upon their physical death, they will most assuredly see what I mean. The followers eventually succumbed to the madness of their leaders, since they feel they have no voice in the affairs of their life, so they merge their voice with that of their leaders. To these followers death is their final statement. Some cultures believe that a martyr's death is a holy thing. In fighting for their distorted religious beliefs and the mass beliefs of the members of their organizations, they perpetrate their madness upon the rest of the world, again feeling fully justified in doing so. An effective brainwashing indeed to allow for the leaders to fully carry out their plans of attempting to make the world conform to their beliefs, all in the name of God.

*Hitler was another example
of a paranoid fanatic going awry...*

The Cult's Inception

You have a natural response to the thoughts of others though and generally speaking have built-in protections from becoming entranced in another's beliefs. It is only those who feel that they have no power of their own who fall prey to the belief systems of others. Those are the ones who would rather give the responsibility of their thinking to someone else rather than confront their own conflicting sets of beliefs. Oftentimes as these individuals move away from the mainstream of religious indoctrination they get caught up in fanatic cults that your societies have been experiencing in recent years. Their ideas and thoughts attempt to move as many minds into the realm of their thinking, thus removing them from the mainstream of society. Once removed from the mainstream the leaders then have complete control over the ideas and movements of their followers.

Fear is the primary tool that these leaders use to keep their followers in the group. The other is rewards, rewards that they believe and are convinced of by their leaders, that they will most assuredly obtain when they give up their lives for the movement. Most often the followers will abandon everything in pursuit of these new sets of beliefs. As the followers grow in numbers, the beliefs are then reinforced stronger until the point when the rest of the world is perceived as the enemy, the enemy that does not understand their perceived enlightened state of being, because this is how most if not all see this new revelation of experience. Since it is not the norm for the rest of society, then it must be something new for only the chosen to experience. These individuals perceive themselves as the new leaders of the pack, out to manifest the ideas of their leaders as good little soldiers would do. They become so entwined in these new sets of beliefs and often they will fight to the death to get the distorted point of their idealistic leaders, and now themselves, across.

As governments will do, they go in and blow the perceived enemy up, thinking that killing them all off will solve the problem. The belief systems of the people have not been changed though and many more will spawn and continue the movement unless the beliefs of these fanatic individuals can be realigned. If left unchecked and to their own devises these fanatic groups will wreck havoc on the rest of the world's societies. They fully believe that they are justified in using whatever means available to them to get their point across. Hitler was another example of a paranoid fanatic gone awry and the projected mass belief system that was able to sway so many individuals into the realms of his thinking.

Humanity is on the verge of making giant leaps in the further evolution of its souls and is starting to awaken to the systematic indoctrination of beliefs that they have for so long accepted. You can make a difference in this world by telepathically sending messages of love to these individuals. You can surround them and their nations with a ray of The Creator's healing light. As you surround yourself with love light and use your own positive intuitions and abilities, motivated by love for your fellow man to send your messages, you are then making a difference in changing the world for the betterment of mankind. The exercise below can be used whenever you wish to bring some positive healing energy to another.

EXERCISE:
RAY OF LIGHT

This is simple to do and quite effective. Whenever you choose, envision a ray of The Creator's healing bright light beaming down directly on another. You may envision the ray on one individual or many. For instance: when driving in one's car, if you experience a driver under the control of negative energies, envision a ray of this light descending down upon them. Focus all of your energies on sending loving thoughts to that person and surrounding them with a protective shield of light. Ask that The Creator remove the negative energies away from their soul and heal their thoughts. You may then keep the ray on them for the rest of their day if you wish. Just ask that it remain and it will.

8. THE REALITIES OF A DISTORTED WORLD

Fanatics are inverted idealists with visions of grandeur and an obsessive desire for power...

Idealists and Fanatics

Let us give some thought here to idealism and fanaticism. In a way each being on Earth is an idealist to some extent. Most individuals devote a good portion of their daily lives actualizing their idealized goals. It is most important to be aware of your actions and monitor them on a daily basis to ensure that you're realizing your ideals and that they are in line with the soul aspects of self. It is when your idealism turns into the negative and controlling arena that problems arise. If you are willing to express your idealism at any price to others no matter what, then you have engaged in fanaticism. This can be seen with the leaders of the terrorist's organizations, political leaders, politicians, corporations and religious groups and cults. Anywhere you see a select group of individuals trying to control the masses you will find idealists in some form or another.

Fanatics are inverted idealists with visions of grandeur and an obsessive desire for power. Anyone or thing is dispensable in order to achieve their distorted version of the world. They do not tolerate dissent or opposition to their perceived vision of reality. Oftentimes money is the driving force behind these unscrupulous beings. They perceive money as power, so the more they amass, the more power they feel that they have. All the while, these individuals have had issues with their own lack of power for the majority of their lives. They have decided that mankind is evil and that they are going to take what they can get by whatever means necessary, always justifying their actions in pursuit of their perceived ideals. Ideally there is nothing wrong in wanting to change the world for the better, but when "for the better" comes with unrealistic visions that create fear and cultivate greed and ignore the desire for mankind to experience his soul's essence in a peaceful way, then you have stepped into the role of fanatic.

If you are willing to violate Universal Law and kill one another in the pursuit of peace or your distorted version of reality then you have only perfected the art of killing, not just physical killing, but killing the spirits in the minds and hearts of mankind and animals. There is more than one way to kill, and all of it is a violation. Anytime humanity is willing to sacrifice the lives of beings whether animals, plants or other humans it is a violation. They have lost respect for life of any kind and that in itself is a step towards the further erosion of your environment and your societies. Only when humanity can demonstrate with their actions that all life is sacred and that all living things are part of the Divine energy of The Creator, can you begin to evolve your consciousness.

Your perceived beliefs are what get you into so many wars, unnecessary wars, as all are, for they have no value. You have only succeeded in identifying yourself with a defensive illusion. Both sides are fanatical about their perceived sets of beliefs and are unwilling to tolerate the perceived beliefs of the other. Now, the terrorist organizations that your world is currently experiencing are a matter of great concern to Beings of Light, for they are truly influenced by negative energies and must be dealt with for the peaceful survival of the planet. In your world presently, because of this threat, war has been projected to the masses as the only answer that your governments can undertake. There are other alternatives, though your leaders are unwilling to entertain them. Killing for the sake of peace leaves humanity with a true lack of understanding of peace.

> *He is an idealist and a fanatic, caught up*
> *in his own version of reality the way*
> *he has created it and envisioned it...*

One of the Leaders

I will give you just a small, brief synopsis about one of the terrorist leaders. He often was overindulged, living within the confines of his family "palaces" as he liked to think of them. He maintained much power over the rest of his siblings, often in a very negative light. He realized early on in his adulthood that he was able to manipulate anybody he chose to by virtue of his charm. He set himself out to be very charming for he realized that he had much more control over others using this tactic. He was quite powerful within those structures in his own right; however this was not enough to satisfy his enormous appetite for power and ego-gratification.

The unfortunate thing about this individual is that he so easily manipulates others with his charm and leads others down this same path of self-destruction. He was not pleased to be exiled from his home base and took on a vengeance that he swore he would make others pay. He is an idealist and a fanatic, caught up in his own version of reality the way he has created it and envisioned it. He has been ostracized by most of his closest relatives and his behaviors are abhorrent to most of his family and that further enrages this being. He is now so obsessed with the power of getting his point across and regaining the power that he feels that he lost, that he will use whatever means necessary at whomever's expense to justify the means. He has assumed a self-righteous attitude now, masquerading behind the guise of religion and convincing his followers that he is the right hand of Allah. Because of the great wealth of this individual, he has latched himself onto a nation of people in turmoil with false promises under a religious mask.

Understand, his followers were in and are in a situation where they feel helpless and any answer to the current plight of the people is going to be a welcome one even if it entails mass killings. Since the people of this nation do not trust the leaders of the Western world along with other nations of power, and rightfully so, they will turn to one of their own for answers whatever those answers may be. The Middle East has been known by all in the Universe as one of the vortexes of the negative entities. It is going to be a great struggle to release these nations from the grips of this reality and change their way of thinking. No matter how many bombs your nations drop, the ideas and the movement have infiltrated all aspects of society in all nations to some degree or another. When the belief systems are aligned with the will and plan of The Creator, you will have peace.

CHAPTER 9

The Forces of Power

The Negative Media | Government & Man's god |
Religion & Government | The Western World Government |
Terror & Fear

*Your media could be used as effective tools
with the right intentions to fight your war on terrorism
without having to kill anyone...*

The Negative Media

The world's media - through television, movies and the printed word - all have some dark content to serve up to you on a daily basis. Most of the individuals presenting this information to you have no clue that they are being systematically controlled by negative energies. They merely think that they are providing a service or filling a need for the insatiable appetite of your society's obsession with violence. The soul-you is not used to this kind of stimuli when not in incarnation, where everything in your home dimension is in harmony. This kind of stimuli is shocking to the soul and in a way you are curious as to the affects of what watching violence does to your physical body as it increases your adrenaline output, a purely physical sensation that itself is a high for you. As adrenaline increases, the natural reaction afterwards is a calming effect. Your society seeks this stimuli in an effort to "experience," for your natural impulses to experience your life have been put to a halt, so you must seek other forms of stimuli to experience. All too often this comes in the form of negative, violent media productions.

If you will stop and take notice, a heartfelt movie or an experience where you have done something kind for a stranger will produce the same effects, but you ignore it, considering it not fashionable. You have succumbed to the will of the negative influences and your ego. It is not healthy for the mind, body and spirit of mankind to indulge itself in this kind of programming. You set yourself up to fall into the belief systems of the negative influences. Take for instance your news stations. They rarely give you any good news and if they do, it is some human-interest story as filler for their regular programming. The brunt of the programming of your minds (humorously) is in the negative arena, supporting your fears and outright encouraging them. Your media have very effectively turned your societies into fear-based societies. It seems as though no news is good news unless it's bad news. You can change this. You do not have to accept a steady diet of negativity and fear. It is most detrimental to your psyche and your being as a whole to indulge in this kind of stimulation. It robs you of the true fulfillment of your soul's purpose and interaction with the rest of humanity. It sets you up to distrust and fear the beings that you have incarnated with to experience your planet.

Your media could be used as effective tools with the right intentions to fight your war on terrorism without having to kill anyone. Given the right kind of information, humanity could elevate its consciousness quite willingly. I am often perplexed as to why this valuable invention of yours (television) has not been used to its greatest potential for the good of humanity instead of promoting negativity and fear. It is one of your greatest sources of power, yet it is used unwisely to convey messages that do not further the evolution of the soul in any way.

As governing bodies became larger and larger,
so did mankind's problems...

Government and Man's god

Let us talk about governments and man's god. Man's consciousness has always identified itself with the physical body first. Somewhere along the line, in developing the awareness of his being, the perception of time, birth and death became somewhat distorted. In the beginning of his evolution, he was less aware of a time/space constraint. His natural relationship with the Earth and his original awareness of his creator were all he needed. Eventually though, that awareness was replaced with his newfound beliefs. He had created for himself a god of man that would be the prime director of his life. He had been fully aware that his consciousness and that of animals were working in harmony towards their own individual evolution. For both understood that their actions, whether prey or aggressor, were fulfilling the needs of each other's species and guaranteeing their survival. Again, I am using "he" and "him" here only as a reference to encompass all humans within the framework of these writings, since the soul has no gender.

Mankind has always felt that within his greater being he was to have some controls put upon him for whatever reasons. He was unable to accept the idea that his being would and could fully experience itself under its own power. His limitations set him apart from other creatures. Instinctively, in the beginning of his soul's evolution he was more aware of himself. As time passed though, in his eyes he became frightened of himself and his curious impulses. He felt the need to control his nature. Mainly through superstitious beliefs and then the creation of his various versions of a god, he became further and further ensconced in the beliefs that there was some part of his nature that he could not control. He felt that it was best to hand over the power to other authorities that would then oversee his life and ensure that he was keeping himself in line with his ideals.

In the beginning, governing bodies were relatively simplistic and as behaviors changed so did the consequences. The very idea of being governed started to erode at his natural impulses to experience his creaturehood. He started to become fearful and acted out in all different manners to try and regain what he had given up. Soon there were many rules and laws, because behaviors became increasingly unpredictable and members of society felt the need to have their governing bodies impose more restrictions. From the beginning of time on your planet there have always been leaders in some form or another, just as there is a hierarchy within the packs of animals. Man too aligned himself with the idea that it would be far better to have someone in charge, thus relinquishing the power of his individual nature to someone else. As governing bodies became larger and larger, so did mankind's problems. More restrictions forced his being to lash out with all sorts of distasteful behaviors. However since this was his creation, he was going to have to live with it. A governmental body was widely accepted by the masses that thought it much easier to have someone else deal with society's ills than have to confront these issues on an individual basis.

Mankind's ego needed to feel that it was still
in control of itself, so it imagined for itself
a god of man...

Religion and Government

The religious organizations man had envisioned to feed his need for spiritual growth were unwilling to deal with society's legal problems. It became easy for him to shift the blame onto a law and thus not have to deal with the issues personally. For it is the law and the law must be followed and so on it went, never realizing that he was systematically cutting himself off from experiencing the nature of his being which is basically good. With all of his pent-up anger and frustration, he was starting to experience another side of himself that he did not understand and became fearful. Of course even before his creation of a government, he had always aligned himself with a God-force. The concepts of a God have always paralleled the ideals established within the governmental structures.

Mankind's ego needed to feel that it was still in control of itself, so it imagined for itself a god of man, a god that took on the characteristics of man and would be a god of power. This concept was most important to mankind's developing ego and ideals. Many nations have formed their own idealized version of god, and oftentimes the majority of their wars were fought in the name of God. With the emergence of this human-like god who was given the power to punish man for his perceived good and evil, came various forms of religion, many using fear as a tool to gain control of mankind's soul.

Governments also seized upon the moment and in an effort to control mankind began using similar tactics that man has willingly accepted en masse. In the Western world and some other nations a democracy was formed that aligned itself with society's religious beliefs. This was a cooperative effort in order to maintain an accepted equilibrium in society. For some time this system has worked for mankind, however with the awakening of his consciousness he is no longer able to accept the fables and fairy tales of his nature. With religion and its more intuitional knowledge and government with its more intellectual knowledge, mankind was now embarking on a journey of conflicting wills. As your conscious knowledge became more and more available to you, your ego has had to grapple with the old system of beliefs. The realities that you have been ignoring, you can no longer pretend do not exist. As your governing institutions, scientists, medical establishments and religions all mount their efforts to suppress this knowledge, mankind will rise up and expose them one by one. Governing bodies in today's civilizations are of a massive nature. For every infraction that humans have been able to perpetrate, a law has been put into place to stop it. There are always those acting out of their own frustrations that will look for ways to circumvent the system in order to try to regain their power. It has been a fruitless effort at best. However all that is about to change.

so much confusion, it is a wonder that you have not blown yourselves up, for lack of communication alone is of massive proportions...

The Western World Government

The governing bodies of the Western world are in constant conflict amongst themselves. The blame game is masterfully played out within these groups. It is as if the right hand knows not what the left hand is doing and furthermore does not want to know. The conflicts of power are pervasive and cause much confusion within the hierarchies of the system. The system itself is flawed and the cooperative efforts of a few are undermined by the voices of many, all wanting their perceived rightful place within the political power structures. So many conflicting ideas, so much confusion, it is a wonder that you have not blown yourselves up, for lack of communication alone is of massive proportions.

Ideally, when governmental structures were formed, there were only a handful of individuals who were relied upon to make the decisions for all involved. However, with the abuses of power it became necessary for you to install safeguards against this. Your safeguards have all but overwhelmed the system at this point and no one trusts the other. Your governmental systems have been at war with themselves for decades and have terrorized their citizens as well. The negative influences have seen to it that there is much strife between the ranks and they have been cleverly putting their people into place to further undermine the system. In the Western world and in the democratic form of government, there is much freedom within the structures to allow for free expression of ideas. When there are so many leaders and so many different ideals wanting to manifest themselves, it is hardly a wonder that you are unable to get much accomplished. Your government leaders spend an inordinate amount of time going in circles.

9. THE FORCES OF POWER

*The human factor has been removed
in favor of profitability...*

If you are to have an effective governing body, it must be done without the influences of your corporations and political posturing on the part of individuals with less than honorable intentions. In most societies, money is always at the root of all decisions. The human factor has been removed in favor of profitability. The average citizen in the Western world has very few choices about how too experience his life because he has allowed his governmental bodies and religious organizations too much control over his being. You have become complacent to the atrocities prevalent all around you, taking them for the norm. Again, not wanting to exert your power, you leave it up to others, who it is well-observed, do not always have the best interests of humanity in mind. The Western world has become so complacent that they will take almost any form of abuse, whether it is taxes, corporate abuse, medical abuse, political abuse etc. You wonder why then that you have been attacked by terrorists. Had you not been asleep, this would not have happened. Had each and every one of you actively taken an interest in the plight of humanity, this would not have happened. Had each and every one of you not ignored each other, this would not have happened. Had each and every one of you taken the time to love and respect each other, this would not have happened. Had each and every one of you cared about what was going on around you and became involved in the betterment of your fellow human beings, this would not have happened. This was a wake-up call to all of humanity even though it happened on American soil.

Mankind is now on the threshold of fulfilling his spiritual abilities and experiencing the magnitude of self. By realigning your thoughts, not denying your greater reality and regaining your individual power, you are going to effectively begin to change your consciousness. This does not have to take on a violent nature to happen, nor does one have to use drastic measures to make a point, for all messages are better received when they are delivered with love. Focus on changing your reality one step at a time, starting with your individual personal experiences on a daily basis. When you have cleaned up your own houses, then you will be free to experience your soul's true essence and creativity and begin to help others. No matter how small you think your voice is, it is always heard and in the realms of the higher-dimensional beings, we hear your calls and they will not go ignored.

This is a very tumultuous time for mankind indeed as the negative energies are being exposed...

Terror and Fear

I would like to speak about terror and fear, mankind's biggest hurdles to overcome as he moves into this next phase of his evolution. Those who want to terrorize humanity are most resistant to change. The ideas and fanatical behaviors of groups or individuals that wish, for their own sake of power, to take away the free will of others is a real threat to humanity. Mind/thought empowerment of fear puts one in the defensive mode and once there terrorism becomes justified. Those who have empowered fear will terrorize others and entire nations in an effort to suppress the evolution of souls. As the consciousness of mankind moves forward these negative forces will resist.

The Earth's inhabitants are evolving and with that evolution many events such as 9-11 will present themselves. Humanity is being given great opportunities to diffuse situations that would otherwise lead to your own destruction, through the thoughts and actions you manifest at this time. The brave souls who unconsciously and unknowingly gave their lives in the 9-11 event did not sacrifice their lives in vain. These human beings gave their lives so that the rest of the world would wake up and start to evolve its consciousness and put an end to terrorism, fear and separation.

Earth is moving towards the light. This is happening now. This has always been a probable reality, but at this time, in your timeframe as you know it, the time is now, it has begun. The ones in power are losing their power one by one. Darkness is moving into light. The portals of the negative energies in the Middle East are extremely active at this time as they make their final attempt to try and prevent the awakening of mankind. Many of you are awakening though and exposing the negative influences for all to see. These forces that have kept mankind in the dark for so long are now being confronted by the awakened ones. This is a very tumultuous time for mankind indeed as the negative energies are being exposed and you witness the crumbling of your corporations, religious organizations and the very structures of your societies. As the negative forces crumble in your society, so it is that they will fall throughout your world.

The Middle Eastern terrorists understand
that death is not final, so they play upon
your fears of death in the Western world...

Mankind is now moving rapidly towards the awakening of his soul and the vast acceleration of Earth into alignment with the vibrational frequencies of other galaxies is coming into awareness. Your preconceived notions that you will be destroyed or annihilated are the life force, food so to speak, that feeds the fear. I ask you this, "What happens to anything when the food is taken away?" It dies off and its energy cannot sustain itself on the physical plane. When you conquer fear, it is to embrace it with love. For where there is love, there is no fear. Fear is a projection of your thoughts and imagination manifested into your reality.

When mankind fully understands death and embraces it for what it truly is, there will also be no fear of death. Your life on this planet is like a play, a script that you have written to further evolve yourself. You all have done this thousands of times in thousands of ways. When you are able to embrace the true nature of your soul and open your minds to the fullness of your being, you will understand and there will be no more fear. Fear is what has kept humanity locked outside of itself for thousands of years. There are so many fears that have been injected into the minds of humanity to prevent you from experiencing yourself.

Death is only a transition from the state of being as you know it with your dense body to light-body existence. You simply do not die. I cannot tell you this enough. Your physical body, your vehicle, when you no longer need it and have learned what you came here to learn this time, simply surrenders itself to another life form. All of the molecular energy of the physical body simply makes the transition of its energy into another life form. You are the driver of this vehicle and as the etheric soul that you are, you simply move out of the driver's seat and back to your home dimension without your vehicle. Plain and simple. It is not necessary for you to place a multitude of fears upon yourself, especially when it comes to death as you think of it.

The Middle Eastern terrorists understand that death is not final, so they play upon your fears of death in the Western world and are very successful at terrorizing you because of your perceived understanding and beliefs about death. However I will make a point here, they are quite misguided as well, for their beliefs about death and martyrdom go against Universal Law. They are in for a big and quite unpleasant surprise when they attempt to cross over into their home dimension.

It was intended for souls when incarnating into the physical plane to experience it, yet because of your beliefs, most of you have not experienced it at all. You all have mastered the art of fearing and thus with your beliefs have terrorized yourselves. You blame the terrorists for terrorizing you when it is your own set of beliefs that has allowed you to be terrorized. The negative influences know this. They know humanity is weak when it comes to your understanding of yourself and the true nature of your soul. All of humanity, plants and animals experience the transition of their energy from one life form to another. You have spent much time prior to experiencing this current life and others from past and future timeframes, carefully choosing the scripts you wished to experience. You have been in many plays of life on many planets other than Earth and in a multitude of timeframes. It is not to fear, but to embrace. Know that you are in the play, the script you wrote to experience life, and when that act is over you move on to other realms of your evolutionary path.

CHAPTER 10

The Multidimensional Reality of the Soul

Simultaneous Lives | Simultaneous Lives Diagram |
Other Selves & Other Realities | Your Inner Reality |
Exercise: Healing Your Other Selves | Your Life Plans |
Thought Reality | Ego vs. Soul & Soul Validation |
The Walls of Separation

*All is possible, yet you have focused on your
perceived reality as the only one you have
or will ever have. It is simply not the case...*

Simultaneous Lives

Some of you may not understand how you can live many lives at the same time. I will try to explain. The energy of your self that encompasses the greater portions of the actualized self is capable of branching-out portions of itself into other lives to experience them. You have an infinite amount of energy that you could be using to achieve this. The physical manifestation of self in your timeframe is only but a minute portion of the totality of who you are. The diagram that I drew up to help you focus on your point of power would somewhat illustrate this. As always, you choose how many lives you wish to experience at any given time. Each time your energy makes the transition from a physical body to your home dimension, some of that energy is returned to the whole if you choose. You may bring as much energy as you feel that you need into each life. This would be evident in some of your great leaders, who have brought greater amounts of energy into those lives because it would be needed to accomplish their objectives.

If you can envision this clearly, you all experience lives in the same way as that of The Creator, distributing different portions of your total energy into different lives to be experienced whenever and however you wish. When Cas, who is now in a female vehicle, is communicating with this portion of the Seth entity, of whom I am and he is a part of, Cas has learned to tune-in in a manner of speaking and let the information from myself come through just as my first subject did. We used a variety of techniques in the beginning, starting with hypnosis, and then eventually he was able to allow me to communicate without the hypnosis in the traditional sense. Now he stays in a focused state of concentration as I communicate with him and through him. It is somewhat like a mental veiling as he is aware of my presence as I mentally imprint thoughts to him or speak through the use of his vehicle. It is also quite possible for you to experience more than one life in a given timeframe. My first subject and Cas are examples, both having an incarnational body within some of the same timeframes I am communicating with, yet separate souls on different aspects of the evolutionary path. Of these simultaneous lives, some portions may be in one part of the world living out their lives, while others that you are quite unaware of, may be living out their lives in another part of the world or even on other planets for that matter. All is possible, yet you have focused on your percieved reality as the only one you have or will ever have. It is simply not the case.

The following illustration will help you visualize the concepts I have presented here in its very limited sense as there is far more to the greater reality of self than this limited diagram. Envision the total energy of yourself as you branch out to all of your simultaneous incarnational lives. The diagram illustrates envisioning a matrix of energy as the main portion of your soul's energy, the portion that you have brought into this life and the other portions in your other simultaneous lives that you are not focusing on in this current life. You are at present using a portion of your energy to focus in this timeframe. All of your simultaneous lives are still continuing to exist. If you wish to affect them, you will need to focus on sending your healing energies from this point of power to them. In doing so, you are able to branch out to the rest of your lives, thus affecting your past, your present and your future. The information that you send in a positive light with an abundance of love, will affect those lives in a most beneficial way and further your own spiritual evolution.

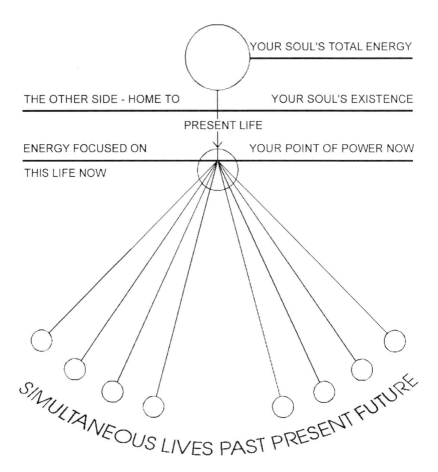

YOUR SOUL'S TOTAL ENERGY

THE OTHER SIDE - HOME TO

YOUR SOUL'S EXISTENCE

PRESENT LIFE

ENERGY FOCUSED ON

YOUR POINT OF POWER NOW

THIS LIFE NOW

SIMULTANEOUS LIVES PAST PRESENT FUTURE

FROM YOUR POINT OF POWER NOW, YOU ARE ABLE TO DIRECT YOUR THOUGHT ENERGIES TO THESE OTHER LIVES, AFFECTING THEM AS WELL. SEND YOUR MESSAGES TO ALL OF THEM IN A LOVING WAY. THIS WILL GREATLY ENHANCE YOUR SOUL'S EVOLUTION AND THE EVOLUTION OF YOUR PLANET INTO THE PEACEFUL FOURTH DIMENSION. DO THIS IN MEDITATION FOR FIVE MINUTES THEN MOVE ON WITH YOUR DAY. DO THIS DAILY. THIS POWERFUL EXERCISE WILL ENHANCE YOUR LIVES AND OPEN YOUR CONSCIOUSNESS TO THE GREATER REALITY OF YOUR BEING.   *~ Seth*

You are always learning from the experiences
of your other selves as well as your probable selves...

Other Selves and Other Realities

Oftentimes in the dream state other realities will be revealed to you and in the dream state you communicate with your other selves all of the time. You are not able to focus on more than one timeframe for very long though in the waking state, due to the portions of the brain that you refer to as gray matter. Certain portions of the brain could handle the simultaneous material, but only for a limited time. In other words, you cannot live and experience all of your lives at once in your dream/waking state in your current physical body. With the expansion of your consciousness these areas of the brain are being activated. It is quite possible for you to experience some of your multiple selves with meditation and hypnosis. Some individuals are capable of tapping into past and future lives as you think of them in the hypnotic state. You are always learning from the experiences of your other selves as well as your probable selves, your probable selves being the thoughts and impulses that you did not act upon. Even though you did not actualize those thoughts with your actions in this point of power, nevertheless they are real and are still being carried out in the same manner that your life is as you know it.

Let me give you an example here: suppose at a young age, you are a woman or maybe a man and you either had a child or fathered a child. Then that child either died or maybe was given up for adoption. Either way, you were not part of the child's experience whether it lived or died. However, that experience still lives on as a probable reality that you did not manifest into action but nonetheless the energy of the thoughtform still continued on. If you want to experience that probable reality for yourself in this point of power, imagine to yourself starting at the beginning of the experience when you made whatever decision you made. Only this time imagine what would have happened if you had made another decision. Now you are experiencing another probable reality within your life that you did not actualize into form in this point of power. You can take this as far as you want to and eventually it will lead you to another probable outcome of one of your probable selves. These probable selves are all extensions of your consciousness. They are experiences of your greater energy source that you have not focused on or acted out in your present point of power. However, they are as valid as the present focused reality in which you are engaged as you read this material.

Now, your conscious mind and your biological nature are of one. They cannot be separated and they function harmoniously together. The thoughts of your conscious mind directly affect your biological self. Your conscious mind directs the activity of the self and allows it the freedom to move around in your environment. It is the directive needed to maintain your existence from millisecond to millisecond. All the cells in your body rely on it to carry out their orders for your state of being. So do your thoughts, for they also have the impetus to seek out their own fulfillment. They are expressed through your desires to make them into your reality, to experience them through the creative development of your creaturehood. As the cells in your body respond to the stimulus of your thoughts and the manifestations of your actions, you are co-creating your reality with the many probable realities available to you, thus expanding your consciousness. Since you have free will, you will only experience and believe what you want to, but as you awaken to the endless possibilities of your reality you will be presented with a greater challenge to those beliefs. You will be opening the doors to the vast richness of your being and in doing so other areas of self will start to unfold and reveal themselves to you.

If you did not feel the need to manipulate and destroy your outside reality and instead focused on the wisdom of your inner reality, there would be no need for wars or devastation on your planet...

Your Inner Reality

In coming together as a species, not as a race or races, but as humans together in a collective consciousness for the happiness and health of all and acceptance of all, the alignment begins and so does the healing, the healing of the wounds of mankind from the separation of selves. There is no separation from you and every living thing throughout the Universes and the consciousness of All That Is. The God consciousness is within you, not outside of you the way you believe it to be. It is internally integrated into every cell of your being. It cannot be removed and set up on a cloud to look down upon you in judgment of you. The only judgment comes from self's limited perceptions of who he is and his expectations of self based on the acceptance and opinions of others. As one breaks away from his exterior reality and belief systems and starts to focus on his inner reality, he will find most if not all the answers that he is searching for. In a way, the inner reality provides all the stimulus and information you need to experience the outer reality. You do not need interference of external stimuli that is not grounded in the fulfillment of the happiness of the soul. In discovering the scientific facts about your biological nature, that you hold to be the reality of your being, external stimuli so to speak, you remove yourselves farther and farther from the knowledge you so desperately wish to attain. That knowledge lies within the consciousness of every living thing, not within the physical framework. When you truly understand the uniqueness of consciousness, then you will begin to experience the answers that you are searching for.

If you did not feel the need to manipulate and destroy your outside reality and instead focused on the wisdom of your inner reality, there would be no need for wars or devastation on your planet. You would be consciously in balance with nature and all living things including yourselves.

At one time on this planet this is how you lived in your ancient civilizations, but you grew away from this in pursuit of other stimuli. You essentially threw yourselves out of balance and have been trying to get back ever since. When reading this material, it is my sincerest desire that all of you will begin the awakening and start to enjoy the benefits of the vast library of knowledge that is inwardly available to you and start to look at your lives with a renewed interest in your planet and the other life forms that have so willingly sacrificed their lives for your unnecessary pursuit of external knowledge. All the answers lie within. All you have to do is listen. Below is another exercise to assist you in understanding and healing other portions of your energy.

EXERCISE:
HEALING YOUR OTHER SELVES

If I may ask you to look at it in this light: imagine yourself standing in front of a large wall approximately thirty feet long and fifteen feet high. Now, on this wall starting from the left and moving to the right are markers, say every two inches, stacked in rows with approximately one foot between them from upper to lower. The wall may have several thousand markers. To make this simple we will say one thousand markers. Each marker is a life play that you wish to experience with a script of probable realities co-created by you and others. They do not necessarily have to be experienced in any order. Starting at the top left end would be timeframes from your past as you perceive it and move progressively to the right and across and then down again and across always moving to the right. Each move to the right moves into a timeframe ahead of the one prior and eventually far into the future as you perceive it, say thousands of your years ahead of your life as you know it now. What I want you to do in this exercise is focus on your point of power in this timeframe. I would like you to send thoughts of loving and healing energy to all of the markers on the wall. These markers again represent lives that you may or may not be participating in. The idea here is to use your point of power in the NOW to heal your simultaneous lives and bring them into the light.

This wall also represents the many lives available to you when you make the transition of your energy from the Earth plane to the home dimension where you did your life review. As I mentioned earlier, you enter through a holographic matrix into several of those lives to determine the ones you would like to incarnate into. This happens more than you are aware of as souls step into probable lives on your Earth planet. They are able to manifest themselves briefly into lives through the use of the hologram. It is only an illusion to the souls already on Earth when they appear, but nonetheless quite real within the framework of illusion on the Earth plane. When the soul sheds the body of a life completed, the soul may choose any of the other lives that he has carefully created to experience. It is like going to school, one grade completed and then you move on. So it is with the life and death experience of soul.

You may, as you look at this wall, go back or forward in time to experience these lives, since there is no time outside the framework of the Earth plane. Timeframes were set in place for the benefit of soul on Earth. It would be too much for the soul's <u>total</u> energy to focus on experiencing just one of the lives at one time. The total sum of energy of your being would be too much for one physical body to withstand. The soul focuses a portion of its energy in as many lives as it chooses, each one focusing on its own point of power in that timeframe to fully experience that life and in doing so is constantly altering the experiences of the other lives. The other selves are not aware of it consciously, however all influence each other's experiences.

Sometimes you incarnate with other portions of yourself ...simultaneously living together in the same timeframe and often in the same family...

Your Life Plans

There are many probable realities in each life and you will choose those you wish to manifest as your perceived reality in any given life. The other probable realities will still be experienced, but you will not be focusing on them. For instance, when the lessons of your current life are learned and experienced, they can be done with if you choose not to experience them again. Some of those same lessons will be written into other lives as well. Since those lessons were learned and experienced, they no longer need to be manifested in the other lives. Usually you will incarnate into a life with at least three or four lessons that you wish to master the learning experience from. You have free will and since there are thousands of lives to choose from, you may choose to focus on another life or lives with a completely different set of circumstances. All choices are made by you with your free will.

Oftentimes there will be counseling from the elders of the Council as to which life would be appropriate for this portion of your energy to focus on the next time around, but even that is only advice and you will always have the free will to choose. You do not have to focus on each and every one of the thousands of lives you have set up for yourself unless you choose to do so. Others may take your place if you wish to abandon one or many. You may also do the same with other's probable lives and step into situations that other souls have abandoned. Most often this interplay is contained within the soul groups that you usually incarnate with. The majority of your life experiences are experienced within that same group, switching back and forth as mother, father, child etc. Many of these lives you have already focused on and experienced at this point in your evolution, so you will choose from the remaining ones where certain lessons and experiences still need to be mastered.

In gaining a clear understanding of the life/death process, mankind can erase his fears and embrace the transition of his energy with love. Your loved ones will be with you in what seems to be the blink of an eye when you are

158

not in a physical body and have returned to your soul's home. Earth lives are quite short because of all the negativity and stress associated with your current evolutionary aspect of the Earth plane. It is necessary, for the soul would be too traumatized if life were any longer and would not wish to experience other lives. Many times this happens and the soul will wait what appears to be hundreds of Earth years to enter into another life or lives to focus upon.

These situations are never unplanned, they are part of the will and plan of The Creator. Every probable reality in each life is planned with all involved within the group and even outside of the group. You share your lives with many of the same souls over and over again, for these souls are the ones closest to you and you all have agreed to experience these lives together to learn. Sometimes you incarnate with other portions of yourself incarnated with you, part of your total energy. Simultaneously living together in the same timeframe and sometimes in the same family, lessons are learned, so to speak, through yourself, with yourself. What you perceive to be your worst enemy may just be a part of your total energy and another extension of you.

As you look at others, you may be looking at a reflection of yourself and at yourself. All is possible. Your energy is a very minute part of the infinite energy source of All That Is, nonetheless enough for this vast energy source to experience every emotion and life experience. No two souls will experience the same situation in the same way. Each will have its own interpretation of the experience even though the experience may appear to be identical. The energy of All That Is therefore is experiencing every facet of humanity and of other Universes through the manifestation of its energy into souls.

Each time you catch yourself harboring negative thoughts, be consciously aware of them and remind yourself that you are working towards eliminating this kind of thinking...

Thought Reality

As mankind desires tranquility and love on his planet so it will be brought forth. As you change your reality with your thoughts and abandon your fears, you will no longer be terrorized. Your thoughts are the most powerful energy in all of creation for they create your experiences. They initiate the thrust of action on your part and manifest your experience into your reality. Knowing this, understand that your reality is what you create. The manuscripts of your religions project onto you the visions of heaven and hell. Mankind's heaven and hell are his own projections of actualized thoughtforms manifested into reality on the Earth plane. It is what he creates for himself through his thoughts and actions that will determine his beliefs about his reality and whether he is living in his hell or his heaven. What you manifest through your thoughts and beliefs you create for your perceived reality. It's that simple. If you wish to live in fear and terror, you will. If you wish to live in joyous harmony with your planet and its beings, you will. Since you are moving into the unity of consciousness dimension, what you manifest by virtue of your thoughts will be instantly created for you. This is why it is imperative that your thoughts be purified. If you move into this dimension with thoughts of fear for example, then your fears will instantly be manifested into your reality. For some of you this could appear to be very frightening depending on what you have envisioned for yourselves. Each time you catch yourself harboring negative thoughts, be consciously aware of them and remind yourself that you are working towards eliminating this kind of thinking. This isn't going to happen over night, however with repetitive conscious reminders to yourself in each instance it will start to manifest itself into your daily reality. Before too long you will respond with positive thoughts to situations instead. For instance, someone may cut in front of you while you are driving and because of your old conditioning you may feel that they did it deliberately or whatever. Instead you may say to yourself, "This person just didn't judge the distance too well or maybe they are a new driver." A harmless positive thought instead of an angry negative thought. That's all it takes to start reconditioning your thoughts. Granted there will always be some situations that will be hard to justify and you will have to do your best to find some good in it.

If you observe other individuals, you will notice that there are always some people who are happy, no matter what. It is because they have not subscribed to the fear-based belief system of your world. They have decided that they will experience their lives joyously and they will not let fear grip their reality. They are in control of their thoughts and most often negative thoughts would not even enter into their thinking. They will most often see only the positive outlook to any situation even if they have made it up in their minds. These individuals have already evolved themselves into a fourth-dimensional consciousness in many ways. They are walking among you. When you meet one of them you know it immediately because you are most likely drawn to them. They make you feel good and you like to be around them. They validate you and show their love for you without prejudice or fear of rejection. This is what it will be like for all of you in this dimension where there is no fear and no terror. Life will be joyously experienced for the happiness of all as your soul was meant to live. You will begin to learn the art of cooperation with others and the wonderful feeling of expressing the Divine qualities of your soul openly to the world.

As fears are erased you will be able to communicate with other Light Beings throughout the Universes and share universal knowledge, for you will understand that The Creator or God if you call it that, wears many outfits, in many colors, to fully experience everything in the Universes that he wishes to. As you grow in the knowledge that is so rightfully yours and reawaken to yourselves, you evolve. If you ignore fear and do not understand and embrace it, then it will grow and become your reality. If you want peace, you will have it. Create it with your thoughts. Believe in it and believe in the power of your being to do so. This probable reality will indeed manifest itself if humanity would consciously come together and make this happen.

The ego is very protective and will deny
the soul's reflection of itself through the body...

Ego vs. Soul & Soul Validation

Now let us discuss the relationship of the ego to the soul. Many of your fears about death are based in the reality of the ego. They have no power in the soul's reality. You have let the ego take control of your knowledge. The ego does not want to die, but the ego is not you, the soul is you. The ego is a manifestation of the mind experience. The ego separates your soul from its development. Consciously, with your perceived sets of beliefs, you have let the ego take over your thoughts. However, soul knows differently and in the dream state is oftentimes living the life that you have consciously denied yourselves in the waking state. Your dreams are a great reflection of the many facets of soul's experiences in this life that you are focusing on and all the others that you are not presently focusing on. Soul travels to all of them, in all timeframes during the sleep state. You are consciously unaware of it, however if you take the time to write down your dreams you may be surprised to see how much they can reveal to you.

The ego is very protective and will deny the soul's reflection of itself through the body. It does not want to acknowledge the soul aspect of your being. It is only concerned with itself and the physical body in which it resides. As you open your eyes and begin to validate you-the-soul, your ego-self will do its best to foil those attempts by reminding you of your fears and doubts. It is a master at trickery and deception for it is ruled by the materialistic forces of dark. For eons your soul has been incarnating over and ever again always striving to reflect itself through the physical vehicle. The ego has stood in its way much of the time. To some degree your physical vehicle needs the ego for it has been useful in your survival. The soul and the ego must learn to cooperate with each other for the good of the total being. When that happens the soul will have finally mastered its vehicle and will no longer need to incarnate into it. That is the goal of the soul when taking on physical incarnations. The lessons you are to learn and experience from are always related in some way or the other to the ego. When the soul has mastered this aspect of its reality it will no longer be tethered to its lower dimension.

As you learn to live your life without fear, then you will truly have started to evolve your consciousness forward...

The Walls of Separation

The ego will do whatever necessary to invalidate the soul for it perceives its very existence to be threatened by the soul. The soul would not behave the way the ego does and it knows this. It is looking for validation in the physical body that it is lacking in the spiritual body. This causes many problems within your soul. Since your birth you have been invalidated in one way or the other. Your religions invalidate you with their dogma that you are sinners, not good enough, unworthy and you have subscribed to these beliefs. The Christ consciousness did not come here to die for <u>your</u> sins. You are not sinners unworthy of living your life. This is man's idea of himself, projected onto the masses through the guise of religion. Your souls are full of love that radiates with brilliant light. The man-made religious beliefs of being a sinner and unworthy invalidate your soul and make you submissive to the will of others. The social structures and peer groups also invalidated you if you did not conform to their perceived sets of beliefs. As soon as you were able to communicate your desires as a child, the invalidation began and continued all through your lives in one form or the other. You are beautiful, bright, loving beings worthy of all that you desire. Mankind builds great walls of separation around himself in the hopes of being invulnerable to his beliefs and fears. Your pent-up emotions eventually must be released and often they are in a variety of ways, either with disease of the physical being or in acts of uncontrolled negative aggression against others. You were not meant to live like this. You have created for yourselves such a whirlwind of fear and anxiety in your every day lives that your life spans have actually shortened. Without the medical advances that your scientists have made to keep you alive longer, many of you would be dying off much younger. It is quite possible for humans to live hundreds of years in future lives on the planet after you have mastered your fears. Your stress levels will be greatly diminished and you will be free to experience the beauty of your being and the wonders of your planet, other planets and their life forms. As you learn to live your life without fear, then you will truly have started to evolve your consciousness forward. Trust in yourselves and your future and you will open up to the wisdom of your truth. You will experience peace and joy and you will know the God within you.

EPILOGUE

If mankind would learn to tap into the powers
of his love alone, he would be able to power
every electrical device on your planet...

The Acceptance of Self

Acceptance of self is being nonjudgmental of self. Love and acceptance of oneself will allow you to experience every facet of your being as a delightful experience. You are beautiful magnificent beings, radiating with love. Try as you may to suppress that love during your conscious moments, nonetheless it still flows from your being like a great volcano. Much of the time you are unaware of it and oftentimes afraid of it. You are Divine beings with so much power to love. If mankind would learn to tap into the powers of his love alone, he would be able to power every electrical device on your planet. Your thoughts travel instantly throughout the Universes and contain much energy. In the higher dimensions, we harvest those thoughts and transmit them into energy through the use of crystals, a technology yet unknown to your scientists. Earth will reap the benefits of this technology after its citizens have successfully completed this next phase of their evolution. Until that time it will not be available to mankind.

The energy force of your soul is so magnificent and powerful, yet the majority of you are unaware of it or how to make use of it. Your light shines so brightly and you are all capable of giving and receiving Divine love. As you accept yourselves for the wondrous creatures that you are, an abundance of joy and wisdom will move into your chakras, opening up the channels of divine light. By realigning your perceived sets of beliefs, the abundance of restrictions you have placed upon your self will be transmuted into understanding, thus allowing your being to express itself naturally and freely with much joy and love. As you confront your fears and pain and acknowledge and understand them, you are truly moving yourselves into the marvelous change that awaits mankind as he evolves his consciousness into his new level of awareness. This is your greatest freedom.

In truly loving and accepting yourself and others you move further in your evolution. You are completely worthy of receiving love and giving love, as it is a natural expression of your soul. To break free from the indoctrination of unworthiness, sinfulness and shame is to set the soul free. You are truly using your free will when you are able to break the bonds that have chained your consciousness for so long. What wondrous beings you are. Look at yourselves with great love and tenderness, accepting self, with all your perceived imperfections and looking at those perceived imperfections as tools for experiencing your soul's evolution and you will begin to understand the beauty of your being. Here is a small exercise for you to practice at your leisure. It is designed to help you see the magnificence of your being.

EXERCISE:
LOOK IN THE MIRROR

If you would, just examine your faces in all their splendor and you will see your soul essence shining through, the real you, not the mask that you have been wearing for the acceptance of society. For it matters not what others think of you. The important thing is that you accept yourselves and let your soul's love shine through to others. Just take this moment to study yourself, enjoy yourself and know that you are a marvelous creation. Send yourself loving thoughts of acceptance, for you are you and only you can be you.

As your soul's essence shines through, it will draw others to you, for they will see that you are truly living and experiencing your life in Divine essence. As you begin to have a greater understanding of who you are, so you will also begin to understand the rest of humanity and embrace the oneness of your Divine essence with others. As the vibrational hum of just one of you raises itself, it affects others and offers momentum for mankind to move itself en masse.

To sincerely go forth with love, without fear of rejection,
to just send forth the love and kindness
one small step at a time...

When you allow yourself feelings of love and embrace them, others will abandon their fears in relationships with you and so it is as if you have the domino effect. If each and every one of you were to do this at least once a day to start and then move it up to twice and so on, you would see how the chain reaction comes into play and fears will be knocked down one by one. It is not to go forth with dishonorable intentions and see what one can get, for that only feeds the ego and does nothing to further your evolution. To sincerely go forth with love, without fear of rejection, to just send forth the love and kindness one small step at a time, this truly will move humanity in great leaps in its spiritual evolution. One small kindness, each day, every day to start until the day's routine is filled with kindness of love brought forth. This is the joy that your soul knows and you are then allowing your experiences to come from the soul and not the ego. Your true freedom lies in the knowledge of self, accepting self, loving self and not judging self with lack of understanding, but transmuting your fears and pain into love of self and others.

Mankind is moving from the separation of self into a oneness with the self and the soul. You are entering the culmination of hundreds of millions of years of your evolution from darkness and negativity into the light. You are experiencing some very trying times in this timeframe as you know it. Much of humanity is facing a multitude of fear. But know that even at the worst of times you are only moving further in your evolution. Living your lives in the Now, experiencing every facet of your being, joyously co-creating your experiences with the fullness of the light and wisdom of The Creator is a beautiful thing to behold. Cooperating with and sharing all of the benefits of your planet with each other will be easy for most of you to do and it will bring much peace and tranquility to your planet.

It is not important what the egos of others think of you, for this is YOUR soul's evolution and lessons that you have come to the Earth plane to experience. There is no need to be in judgment of anyone or anything for all souls know the path they have chosen and the reasons they have chosen those experiences. Remember that whatever the experience, it has been chosen by you for you to learn from it. It is hard for many of you to understand the choices of others, but it is not for you to judge without awareness and understanding. For their experiences and lessons belong to them and are to be experienced by them, just as yours are for you. It matters not what tomorrow brings. As you focus on today, embracing and accepting your fellow man, this is where changes begin.

GLOSSARY

All That Is: The energy source from which all life sprung throughout the multitude of Universes, transcending all dimensions of consciousness and being part of all.

Astral Planes: A dimensional level within the grid system of Earth. It is a holding area so to speak, for souls who have not fully made the transition of their energy to their next dimension of awareness.

Chakras: Spiritual points on and around the Astral and physical body that allow for Divine information to be received.

The Council: Members of the Spiritual Hierarchy. Highly evolved beings that advise souls on incarnations for their spiritual evolution.

Christ Consciousness: The evolution of a soul into a dimension of awareness and expansion of consciousness with the inner self realizing its divinity.

Christ Essence: The consciousness of The Christ himself.

Cosmic Consciousness: The consciousness of beings from many dimensions in unity with each other.

The Creator: One whose energy source is found in all living things and is responsible for the creation of Earth and its inhabitants. Also see God.

Dark Forces: Negative energies that roam the Universes in pursuit of their own power to dominate the heavens. Also see Negative Influences.

Dimensions: Points of reference from one reality to the other with different vibrational wavelengths of consciousness.

Energy Personality: A being capable of transferring their thought energy inter-dimensionally to physical beings and sometimes using the physical abilities of those beings for communication.

Entity: Beings not presently manifested on the physical plane. Also known as a spirit.

Etheric Vision: A higher dimensional vision and the vision of the soul.

God: The most common name given on Earth to the energy source responsible for creating your physical being and giving life and validity to your multidimensional self, which is your soul. Also see Creator

gods: Man's own consciousness projected outward into his reality. A self-created projection of his developing ego.

Good and Evil: One of the stages of development of the consciousness dealing with opposites as realities. A conscious creation to give guidelines to the ego.

Harmonics: See Vibrational Hum

Higher Dimensions: Part of the framework of the cosmos. Pure energy and pure thought are experienced here.

Home Dimension: One of the many Astral dimensions based on the evolution of a soul.

Illusions: Thought forms manifested into a perceived reality.

Incarnation: To move oneself into another life experience on the physical plane.

Law of Noninterference: Beings of Light or dark are bound by Universal Law not to interfere with the free will of mankind.

Lessons: Chosen life experiences of the soul for further spiritual evolution.

Light: The Universal knowledge, love and wisdom of The Creator.

Light Body: The etheric body of refined light.

Masters: Light beings who were once incarnated themselves who have moved into the higher aspects of their evolution. They are members of your planet's Spiritual Hierarchy who know the will and plan of your Creator. Also see Spiritual Hierarchy

Peaceful Fourth Dimension: The unity of consciousness dimension. Thoughts and emotions are instantly manifested and all soul memories are revealed. A dimension of pure thought where negativity is not allowed.

Perceived Reality: That which one creates based on ones beliefs.

Point of Power: The alignment of your energies with your inner self.

Reality: That which one assumes to be true based on ones thoughts and experiences. Also see Perceived Reality.

Realm: Similar to a dimension.

Simultaneous Lives: The multidimensional simultaneous experiences of souls in incarnation.

Soul's Light: The etheric light of ones soul.

Spiritual Hierarchy: Beings of Light who have mastered multidimensional levels of experience throughout the Universes and have moved on to higher service in the evolution of all souls. Also see Masters.

Universal Law: The laws of the Universe which protect the will of The Creator.

Vibrational Hum: The resonating sounds of the energies of All That Is on multidimensional levels. Different dimensional levels experience different wavelengths of sound.

Violation: Not in alignment with Universal Law.

Questions & Answers with Seth

Terrorist Movement

Mark - When you talk about the "movement," do you mean the terrorist movement has infiltrated all aspects of society?

Seth - I do. The terrorists focus upon recruiting individuals in societies that are rife with political and economic turmoil. They are quite adept at infiltrating these societies and will go to great lengths to further engage these individuals in acts of violence. They take advantage of already mounting pent-up emotions within these nations. The object is to overthrow the current leadership and replace it with the fanatical ideals of the leaders of the terrorist movements. Oftentimes individuals in these nations are so poverty stricken that any hope for a better future is a welcome one. It is easy for the terrorists to sway these individuals into their system of beliefs by promising them many abundant rewards both in heaven and within the movement. The followers within the movement when participating in an act of aggression are looked upon as heroes to the rest of the group. It is a great boost to their self-esteem, which they have little of, to be revered in this way. The leaders of the group will instill as much fear into their victims as possible and en masse. The movement needs to be in control of the masses in order to appear as if they are the ones in power. When individuals are living on a steady diet of fear, they will do almost anything to make themselves feel better and insure their survival. Many of their victims are terrorized so extensively that they have lost all control over their own lives and must succumb to the will of the ones in power or be killed. The indoctrination of individuals into the movement promises a so-called heaven on Earth and in the afterlife if the rules are followed. The hopelessness of the individual followers see this as the only alternative in their existence. It is a brainwashing on a massive scale and because it is under the guise of religion it is easier to bend the will of the followers. They feel they have no power and therefore within the group, the group has power. The group can perpetrate the acts of violence and no one feels responsible individually because it was done by the group for the cause, whatever that cause may be.

The World Players

Mark - So you are going to include the other players on the international scene, our president and others?

Seth - Correct.

Mark - Leaders of other countries?

Seth - And their belief systems. We are focusing on the Western world right now because Western civilization cannot assume that they are the all-good-doers of the world, so to speak. There are mass amounts of corruption within the ranks of your Western democracy. Most of your nation's citizens are kept in the dark as to what their government officials are really up to. It has been put under the guise of national security, however there have been many atrocities perpetrated under this guise. Many of the government leaders are quite hypocritical in the way they portray themselves, for the vision portrayed to the nation's citizens is not always what it appears to be. In the case of the Middle Eastern movement, they perceive the West as evil and on the other hand the West perceives them as evil. Understand however that these individuals in the Mid East have been killing each other for centuries and to them it has become a way of life and the only way that they know to get their individual points across. I am not condoning it because it is not the way, it is a violation of Universal Law. But then you see that this area has been riddled with negativity for centuries. They have been manipulated by the dark forces for thousands of years. This area is considered to be the dinner table of the dark forces to Beings of Light. There are many forces within that area that are coming into play. It is truly the battle of good and evil in a lot of respects if one was to believe in good and evil. The Western world has a democracy going for it, in that this is the entryway into a peaceful existence. However it can be abused and has been abused as well. Many atrocities have been perpetrated under the name of freedom and democracy, many things that your citizens are unaware of and I am not allowed to speak of. You know it all boils down to, whose way is the right way and is there such a thing as the right way. But with the ending of some things is the beginning of others. And I will leave it at that.

Mark - Well, once again, it's compelling.

Purpose of the Book

Mark - Can you talk a little about 9/11 in a broad sense? It caught everyone by surprise. It caught the whole world by surprise.

Seth - Yes because the whole world is sleeping and many of the world leaders are in denial of what they know.

Mark - OK, sleeping in what sense?

Seth - In their consciousness. The plight of humanity, it still goes ignored by most of the free world. The Western world leaders did not want to deal with what they knew was inevitable. They had been warned many times but refused to listen. There is much that they know yet do not reveal to their citizens.

Mark - I agree. Could you say a little bit more about that?

Seth - The consciousness of humanity has been asleep for far too long. We are desperately trying to awaken the world, however it is not easily done. There were many, many signs that this was going to happen and indeed this was a wake-up call to humanity. The citizens of the Western world have spent an inordinate amount of time in the dark about the plight of the rest of the world. You cannot turn away and ignore the problems of the world and go on as business as usual, pretending they don't exist. Americans live in a very powerful nation and other nations are always seeking assistance from them. They have not always been willing to help so this is what happens when the frustration levels of others get out of control. When a government does go in and give nations assistance it is not without a heavy price to pay for those nations. Oftentimes and in most cases the interest repayment alone far exceeds the money that was loaned. Your governments are taking advantage of the situation of the hopelessness of the people. That is not assistance if it puts these nations further in debt to the world giants. That is extortion at a justified and political level. How can that possibly be helping? If you are going to help a nation then it must be done without attachments. The funds should be given freely so that all nations will be able to share the benefits of the planet, not just those in the rich prosperous nations. The leaders in the powerful nations have the ability to make a difference in the world if they choose to. After 9-11 humanity was awakened to some degree, however it is not enough.

Mark - Can you describe what enough would be?

Seth - Well I think we're going to have to do a book or two or three or four or many more to get the masses to see the problem. In this book I will give the reader tools and information that will stimulate them into looking at their world situation and themselves.

Mark - OK and then how does it work exactly? Is knowledge enough for people? They read a book and then decide it's true and then what?

Seth - Knowledge and experience. You will see as we do the book, that if we can awaken the minds of humanity to awaken their minds to each other, we will have accomplished a great deal right there. You are not going to be able to effect all change immediately. It is a process. However, the process needs to be started. If you do not start the process you will not see any results, other than what you are seeing right now, right now meaning more terrorist activities. Understand, terrorists believe what they are doing is right. You will have to change that belief. And you will have to change your beliefs as well for much of what you are experiencing was brought on by yourselves.

The Council

Mark - You mentioned that you were debating with The Council on what specific information you would reveal in this book. Who would The Council be? I'm just curious.

Seth - The Council members are very highly-evolved beings whose service is to advise others on matters of a spiritual nature and on their chosen path. I generally confer with them on matters of importance that involve Universal Law. To put it plainly, they are highly-evolved, more so than myself. I know you are thinking that I am quite up there but I have much to learn. These are my teachers. I go to them periodically for advice.

Lessons of Love

Mark - What is our main purpose for reincarnating?

Seth - You may reincarnate over and over again through the birth/death cycle until you have learned the lessons of love on your planet and mastered your vehicle.

Mark - Could you elaborate on the lessons of love, what that would mean?

Seth - Souls on your planet are to learn how to reflect themselves through their physical bodies and unite the two

187

together. The process of doing so encompasses the ability to learn unconditional love for each other. When your physical body is a true reflection of your soul, then you will be able to move away from the physical body and use your etheric body. Then one moves out of a third-dimensional reality and into the fourth-dimensional reality. Soul entities have an extreme love for one another. All That Is is the prime source of that love. When incarnating into a body the memories of that love have been put into an amnesia block so that humans can experience and learn all that they need to for the lessons and experiences they wish to take on in their chosen lives. The last evolutionary step that humans went through was the development of the ego. The ego has now served its purpose and the new evolution will involve the soul. Love of your fellow human beings has been pushed aside for the satisfaction of the ego-self. The ego has taken charge of mankind and this is not its place. You will be returning back to the full integration of your soul-self. The amnesia will be lifted in this evolution.

Mark - OK memories of this love have been put into amnesia. Is it possible for a person of my profession to help people remember that?

Seth - Through hypnosis Mark you are able to reconnect the soul essence with the conscious mind. It also takes daily meditation to become fully aware of the soul-self. As one meditates, there is an evolution of the strands of DNA that is necessary to this current evolution of the soul-self. The love that the soul has is a euphoric feeling and when meditating or using hypnosis an individual will be able to cross into that part of self that they have been so long ignoring. Since you are all part of All That Is, The Creator's love abounds you and you are fully aware of this love even at birth. Those memories start to fade as you mature and take on the lessons of your life. If you were to retain those memories, you would not experience the lessons that you have chosen for you would have knowledge of their outcome and not wish to experience them. We have all been where you are in my dimension. You do not attain Light Body status without experiencing the Earth plane or something similar to it as there are millions of other planets that we may choose to incarnate on. Earth plane being one of the most negative and hardest to deal with also has much value in the progression of the soul if the entity soul uses the knowledge that it has gained from experience on Earth wisely. The message is always of love. Now in the past I have elaborated on metaphysics and the energy manipulation that goes on with the physical, mental and emotional body, however I feel mankind needs to go back to the basic lesson of learning how to love one another. Soon your bodies will be of an etheric nature anyway and in that dimension there is a whole other set of circumstances that you will be dealing with. So we must try to get you back onto the path of loving one another and cleaning up your thoughts and beliefs. Granted it is quite hard to love someone who is spitting in your face, however look at the spit in the face as a lesson to be learned. If one does not learn to move away from negativity and hate then one does not evolve. It's that simple. We are all on a path of enlightenment whether in my dimension or in yours. The Earth plane is like a giant theatrical play. There are good players and bad players. The end result must be a love for one another and for the planet. The animals, all beings have a consciousness and feelings whether these are plants, blades of grass, insects etc. Each contains a consciousness of its own. Man would benefit greatly if he would get rid of the idea that he is in charge and everything is dispensable to him, for it is not.

Symbols

Mark - I'm curious about your mention of a symbol in one of our private conversations.

Seth - The symbols...

Mark - Yes, can you elaborate?

Seth - Certainly. Let me begin here by saying, in the transition from one form of energy existence to another, for each life lesson that is completed, a symbol is chosen by you. This symbol is a reminder of the life experienced and generally it relates to the lesson or contract theme as it was completed. For instance, if you came into your life to perfect the experience of humility, and that experience was perfected, then the symbol would be chosen. The symbol is chosen by you, for you and is personal to your soul development. The Council members for example have quite an elaborate array of symbols altogether on one piece, which they wear around their necks. Since these beings have had many experiences, they are quite intricate. The same applies to you. Your symbol is your reminder. Now, when meditating often you will see these symbols, you may wonder what they are. If you look further, you will see that they have to do with lessons learned in previous, past or future lives, since all lives are simultaneous. Now let me make this clear, that the present life as you see it is your current focus, however in meditation you are fully capable of focusing on lives that you deem to be past or future. Often when reviewing ones life before entering into another, the soul will bring forth to the meeting with The Council the symbols of the previous life or lives, as a reminder of lessons learned. All communication being telepathic, the Council will know what the symbols mean and will be better able to advise on a new life experience based on those symbols. The Council is always available to help in these matters in choosing the next group of lessons that are for you to learn. One life is not automatically predetermined to be the life following the previous. In other words, you may choose whatever lessons you are slated to learn in any order in which you want to learn them. Some lessons being very difficult will provide you with a life that is very difficult. Other lessons may come in the form of an easy existence, thus explaining why some entities feel they are overwhelmed and have too much on their plate while others seem to skate through life without hardly a bruise. It is all a matter of when you choose to participate in these lessons and their level of difficulty for your spiritual evolution. If you have had many seemingly trying lifetimes, you may then decide the next incarnation will be more peaceful and restful to you. Now, keep in mind, not all incarnations are on the Earth plane. You may choose to incarnate on a variety of other existence's, solar systems and planets, however most of you will come back to Earth for this phase of your spiritual growth as most of your chosen experiences are part of Earth's solar system and you are part of that Creator's plan. The lessons that you have chosen to learn and the stage of your soul evolution will determine the place in which you will manifest your energy. The Earth's third dimension encompasses your physical type of body which is usually chosen for the experiences needed to evolve at that level. That is not to say that those on other planets do not have a physical body for they do. They are just different than yours because of some of the atmospheric conditions. Regardless, the symbols are many and there are multitudes of them. When referring to The Council for guidance as to what group of lessons you wish to learn in your next incarnation (if you choose to do so) you will refer to your symbols. The more incarnations one takes on and the more lessons completed, the more complex your symbols become. It begins to take on a complex personality of its own so to speak because it contains all your life lessons. It is worn as a medallion would be worn. Does that clear this up for you?

Mark - Well, it brings up a lot more questions but this is intriguing information. Can you give me an example of what a symbol would look like? I'm guessing it has a multi-sensory element?

Seth - It is up to the individual as to how the soul makes the correlation between the lesson that was learned and the symbol that it chooses to associate that lesson with. For instance, you may have a tree or symbol of a tree if that reminds you of something that you learned in the previous existence. This is left up to you because it will make the most sense to you. However we are very familiar with each other's symbols as we see them because telepathically we are able to understand the evolution of each soul based on his symbols. When communing with other souls in your home dimension, as you recognize each other and identify with each other, you also know what each of you has learned in your evolution based on your symbols. We visually can see these as if they were draped around your neck as in a large circular medallion.

∗∗∗∗∗∗∗∗∗∗∗∗∗

Simultaneous Lives

Mark - I'm familiar with the point of power - now - the point of power in the present and how you can concentrate on the positive in this moment. Can you talk about how that affects future lives?

Seth - I will explain. Your point of power is the sum of energy that encompasses your current life as you are now experiencing it. When you engage in sending thoughts of healing to your other lives you are using the energy available to you Now to send messages to those other life experiences. Those other lives are not consciously aware of what you are doing but telepathically they are receiving the thoughts. This healing often affects decisions that they (you) would be making thus altering your experiences. One would hope that those experiences would be for the better and that the lessons chosen in those timeframes would be accomplished. You are also altering your experiences in your now by the thoughts that you are sending to yourself from other portions of those lives. As you raise the vibrational hum of your being through awareness, you affect the outcome of your future experiences. The raising of your vibration also affects the rest of society and helps move the planet and its beings into its next level of consciousness. You are bringing that love-light energy to the future-light because you have the energy available in this point of power to send those thoughts. It is really not about a future life anyway because all chosen lives are based on your soul's evolution. If you are to fully understand this one must move away from the time-constraint thinking for it is not relevant when not in incarnation. I know that you are confused as to how you can live all of these lives simultaneously, but I mentioned earlier they have all been chosen and set up for you to experience. There is no time as you know it in the home dimension of the soul as well as many other dimensions. There are many probable realities involved in all of these lives. The thoughts that you think now, the behaviors that you take on now, the ideas that you assume for your own personal reality affect all of these lives and your evolution. They are not consciously aware of it, however the effect is taking place because they are all part of the same energy essence of you-the-soul. Just as you are not consciously aware of them, they are not consciously aware of you. But the messages that you send back and forth to each other do enter into the subconscious mind and are received, whether or not you are aware of it. Does that clear it up or would you like me to go further?

Mark - Well, yes I'm pretty clear on it but I'm wondering if we shouldn't be ultimately clear with people. I think the idea that people need to grasp is that in this current moment in our reality we have the potential to create the peaceful fourth dimension that we're going to move into. Is that it?

Seth - That is correct. You are beginning the process with your thoughts. As your thoughts move toward the light, the vibrational hum of the beings on the planet and the planet itself will move into the change. As the beings move towards the light - the light being knowledge and information - the DNA within the human being will evolve from the double helix to the twelve strands, each twelve strands corresponding to the twelve chakras. This DNA evolution will affect the twelve, the seven on your bodies and the five around the body. As I talked about earlier, the thoughts of your planet, the energies of all of your beings, create the entire environment of your planet, the weather and all the perceived realities within that system. When the vibrational hum of the masses is raised to its new level of awareness and into the light, the planet is able to evolve with its beings. If you move towards the dark or stay within the dark, no knowledge will be brought forth, because darkness does not allow for information and knowledge. You will remain the same or of a lesser quality than you are presently, "quality" meaning you will not physically or spiritually evolve. You will stay within the confines of the third-dimensional reality. Earth is moving forward. It is not in the throes of the backwards momentum. It is moving forward into its next phase on its evolutionary path. If you succumb to the dark forces, you will only succeed in relinquishing your soul's evolution to the powers of those who wish to repress and confine the very nature of your being. As you move into the light the knowledge that has always been there for you will start to show itself within your being. You will be aware of many things you thought impossible to comprehend. That is the process of moving towards the light, the evolution of mankind's physical being as well as the evolution of his soul. You may be asking, "How do I move towards this light?" Your thoughts are what move you towards the light. If you constantly harbor thoughts of darkness then you will be in darkness. The power is yours. It has always been yours. When you take back your power that you have generously relinquished to other forces and use it for the further evolution of your soul you will have started the process. It is no longer necessary to subscribe to the mass beliefs of the doctrines that have been systematically placed into your being for centuries. You are all starting to wake up, some of you quicker than others. Those of you who resist by your own free will still wallow in your greed and manipulation and stay within the realms of the third dimension, which I might add is going to be quite uncomfortable for you until you too seek the light. Those stubborn individuals will not be allowed to manipulate the minds of humanity much longer. Do you have any other questions?

The Chart on Healing Our Other Selves

Mark - I do have questions about this chart. (reads chart on simultaneous lives)

Seth - Simply visualize. Make it as a fan that comes out in

front of you when you are concentrating and send those energies to those lives. And don't be overly concerned about whether they are received. Just do it and be done with it and move on with your day. It will be done as long as you do it. You interact telepathically with other portions of your energy day and night, you are just not aware of it. There's far more there than you can possibly comprehend in the third dimension but I've made it as simple as possible for the reader to do this. This is you, as you send the energies out to other portions of yourself.

Mark - That is for the book? Great! I think people will really like something they can practice with, a visual, a graphic.

Seth - Correct. You visualize yourself. This is your self that you are focused in right now, in this point of power and you are sending healing energies to all of your lives. You then affect all experiences since they're all related.

Mark - OK I've read your books and I understand how it works. But I think that people reading this book may have some difficulty understanding the concept of changing a past life. Changing the past seems like an impossibility.

Seth - It is only a past in your terms because of your linear thinking and the logic behind the time/space continuum. You are in a timeframe so you constantly consider the past over and done with. The past is not over and done with any more than the future does not exist, for they all exist together. They are all there. There are portions of your energy in each one of those lives, living those lives. Think of it this way: you have set up a variety of different lessons and scenarios with which you want to learn. You've picked various different lives and timeframes that you wish to be born into. For the timeframe of the Earth plane, you need only to enter within that portal of time to begin to focus on that particular life. You are all focusing right now as we speak on this particular timeframe, the events of this part of your world's experiences, the perceived reality of your world I should say without getting too technical here. I want this to be absorbed by the reader in the most simplistic of terms. Now, you have in front of you, lets say, a dozen lives and you've said to yourself, "OK I'm going to choose this one now. Many others are going into this timeframe and I wish to go into this timeframe too. This is the life where I will go to learn the lessons I have set up for myself." Based on your own point in evolution you may enter into that life more highly-evolved than others and use that knowledge to assist in the evolution of the others. You may have chosen experiences in other timeframes prior to choosing that one that were either farther into the future as you know it or farther back. The point is that you choose what timeframes to enter into based on your own personal evolution and what you wish to bring to that timeframe from your base of evolutionary knowledge. Now all of the lives, as I said, are being lived simultaneously. When you are done focusing on one of those lives, you will go back to your home dimension, evaluate the life you have focused on and decide what it is that you needed to learn. Did you learn and experience that and do you need to go back and do it again or can you move on with another lesson in another life in another timeframe on Earth or wherever? You make those decisions. They are all there, but because you only focus the greater ball of energy on one at a time, this is where your point of power is. Now it's not to say that you don't have a point of power in all those other lives, for you do, but you are not aware of them in your present life. You are not aware that you are focusing on any of those lives because your focus is here and now in this timeframe. You are getting thoughts from all of your selves all of the time, you are just not aware of it. The thoughts that you send out now are the thoughts that you wish to affect those personalities in those other lives, to help the evolution of your soul and I want the word help to be underlined. Now does that make sense to you?

Mark - Yes, that's an excellent description.

Seth - Now let me add one thing here. When you are in your home dimension preparing to enter into one of your lives and you did not or were not able to learn the lessons you had chosen, as in the case of suicide, you will go back into that period of time that you have just exited from almost immediately. There is a Universal Law involving suicides, which is only circumvented in very special cases where one was already scheduled to die because of terminal illness. In the case of unjustified suicides, you will go back and be reborn from the standpoint of a baby and you will still be within that perceived reality and belief system of the individuals of that time period from which you just came and you will have to re-experience all over again a life similar to the one you opted out on, until the lessons are learned and the contract fulfilled. Because the evolution of mankind takes on what seems to be a slow process, you might miss out on a few years at best, but you will be right back in the same lessons with pretty much the same identical perceived realities. Due to the accelerated pace of your current evolution, for reasons that I won't go into at present, there may be some changes as to what dimensional-level you will reenter into. Since your planet is in the midst of a massive evolutionary change, many of you will not be returning into a three-dimensional reality. This is all predicated on how swiftly your citizens realign their consciousness. The intense energy being poured into your world at this time by the forces of light is going to dramatically affect your entire world as your planet makes this necessary shift into the unity of consciousness dimension. Many of you will re-enter into that dimension because of this evolution. Many of the souls entering into your world at present through the birth process are already evolved to that level and will be assisting the rest of the world to make the transition and will also help with the restructuring of civilization. I will leave it at that for now.

Mark - I think that would be interesting to the readers to see how… where we're headed. This is assuming that we are evolving into Light Beings. Is that too broad an assumption?

Seth - No, you are evolving into Light Beings. In the fourth dimension your bodies will be lighter and more etheric than the dense physical bodies you have now, "light" also meaning information and knowledge. You will be aware of all your simultaneous lives and their experiences for you will be able to feel them and remember them. It is not to judge them though, but to go forth and acknowledge them for what they are, learning experiences that you wished to learn. Your spiritual knowledge has been kept from you far too long. It is the knowledge that has always been available to you but has been taken from you within your mass systems of belief, through your religions and your governments. I have not intended to put down the religious systems as they have their place in helping mankind, but they have also been great perpetrators of darkness. As you notice with the 9/11 event, the terrorists mask their actions and beliefs behind the label of god and religion. This is true in many aspects of government as well, for they try to keep you in the dark about other beings within the Universe for fear that they will be stepping on the toes of the religious leaders. The forces that are trying to prevent you from gaining your soul's knowledge are busily at work trying to keep you in the dark. They go to great lengths to feed off of your negativity. You can see how they have controlled your media. Unwillingly and unwittingly many souls fall prey to this belief system thinking that they are doing the right thing, when in actuality they are being manipulated by the forces of dark. They have handed over the power of their thoughts to others thus serving up to mankind huge plates of fear and negativity on a daily basis.

The Chakras and DNA

Mark - So reading your material can help people focus on their inner lives, what they can do spiritually?

Seth - Books are necessary because you as a species are very verbal. You still have not developed your use of telepathic communication on a grand scale. Stimulation of thought in reading books does allow for the opening of chakras.

Mark - Can you say more about that?

Seth - The more information or knowledge you obtain, the more knowledge that is given to you. The more aware that you become of your spiritual being, the more of your own knowledge you become aware of. It's an evolutionary thing. As your spiritual knowledge becomes more integrated into your being, your soul evolves. The evolution of your DNA is directly associated with Divine knowledge being given to you. DNA holds within it the coding and information of your history and the blueprint of your Universe. As you accept the knowledge that is being given to you your DNA will evolve and release to you your multidimensional history. The chakras are the energy information centers directly associated with the evolving DNA. As the DNA evolves and moves through your central nervous system it will stimulate the chakras. When your own twelve chakras are stimulated you then will be able to plug into other etheric energy discs in alignment with many sets of twelve centers outside your body. With this evolution the vibrational hum of the species will be elevated. This will propel you into the fourth dimension.

Mark - Can I ask what it feels like when the limiting beliefs are transcended? There's some sort of activity that happens in the chakras when the Divine wisdom is coming. I believe you said we receive it through the pituitary and it's translated there. Is that similar to the experience of "grace" or a corrective emotional experience as we say in psychology?

Seth - Everyone experiences grace all the time. You are a state of grace you're just unaware of it. I don't know if I would use grace per se however let me see if I can put this into terms that the reader would be able to understand. The knowledge starts to flow forth and brings a clearer perception to your soul's being. You just become more intuitive and clear about the purpose of your life and your existence as these chakras open. You are experiencing knowledge that you have already had for millions of years. The reality of your multidimensional self comes to the forefront and you are aware of it and you are able to feel it, all of it good and bad. Your soul always carries with it in your DNA and the very molecular structure of your being all of your memories and knowledge. As this evolution takes place it will be easy for you to access it. Your brain is a virtual computer warehouse of information that you have only very slightly began to tap into. As the DNA is evolved your brain will begin to use its full capacity to process all of its simultaneous experiences and access Universal Knowledge. The knowledge is all there in the DNA. Your scientists cannot see the functions of your brain or your so-called junk DNA, because to them they have to see it to believe it. This so-called junk DNA is what will be activated. Much of this cannot be detected by your primitive scientific measures.

Mark - In the Eastern systems they talk about the seven chakras. There's one above the head, the chakra that connects you to the Divine. There's one down under the tailbone. There's seven of them going up the spine. How do you view this?

Seth - There are twelve. Some of them you are not aware of at this time.

Mark - Are all of the chakras associated with some part of the body, the human body?

Seth - The first seven are points within the human body and the etheric body, access portals if you prefer to use that, where information can be released or obtained. With the evolution of mankind into the unity of consciousness dimension all twelve will be available and as man raises his vibration the DNA is being restructured to the twelve strands from the double helix. If you wish to activate these chakras it is important to meditate and release yourselves from your emotional baggage. You may also opt for hypnosis which for some who find it difficult to meditate can be of much help. You will need to be able to handle the multitude of experience that will be released to you without judgment or fear. The body chakras are as follows: Survival, Sexuality, Emotion, Heart, Throat, Third Eye, and the Crown Chakra. The spiritual chakras outside the body are as follows: number eight is twelve inches above your crown chakra, number nine is three feet above the crown chakra, number ten is the link to the solar system, number eleven is the link to the galactic system and number twelve is the multi-universal link to galaxies beyond your own. It will be anchored in your sun system. As you further evolve as a species more will be added but at this time in your evolution this is all that will be needed.

Emotions and Fear of Death

Mark - Last week in our private session you referred to the connection between emotions and disease and how when this is resolved in the future, somehow our emotions are going to be refined?

Seth - Refined emotions, yes you will no longer operate on the emotional level of fear. The fear is what is going to be removed from you at this time in the evolution of your soul. Fear is the emotion of the dark forces. The dark forces would love to see mankind bathed in a sea of fear. Many, many books have brought to light the evolution of the soul and have thus started to eliminate mankind's fears about his being and about his so-called impending death, because death does not exist. One of the first and biggest steps of mankind is to realize that death is just a transition of his energy from the physical body to another form of energy. You are no more dead now than you will be on the day that you die and "die" meaning the day that your physical body ceases to function. The preservation of the species of mankind is predicated on the knowledge that he will know that he will continue to exist in a peaceful and harmonious environment and that with his very thoughts he will move his species into that peaceful realm. Most of mankind does not want to have to come back and face the negativity and fears associated with your existence right now. As you know, you have chosen to experience these lives and in doing so it

207

would behoove you to experience them in a more peaceful manner than to constantly be fighting for your ego-survival. The negative forces have had such a horrible impact on the physical body and the mass belief systems of the entities on your planet. They have done much to destroy the natural healing processes that the body was built with. If left alone the body is perfectly capable of taking care of itself. It does not need artificial means to stimulate it or to prevent it from doing its job. It was beautifully designed to enhance the experience of the human condition. It was meant to experience all of its parts joyously and freely for the growth and the evolution of the soul.

Mark - Are you going to have an exercise on anger management?

Seth - Anger is a natural emotion. If left unchecked to just allow itself to manifest it will dissolve itself. You need to experience anger to release the energies that caused the anger but in that release you should not be hurting others but instead question why you had the anger. What were the circumstances that caused your perceived beliefs about how and what you expected from the person or persons that you feel caused the anger? Had you set up false perceived realities for yourself and then those realities were not manifested? Did you not get what you were expecting and therefore you lashed out in anger and hurt others because it didn't go your perceived way? It would appear that people or persons are not conforming to your perceived reality. You set yourself up for your own anger. If you would allow others to perceive their reality in their own way and you experience yours in your own way and leave no expectations out there you would be much happier as a species. You would take what you get and be happy and move on.

Mark - OK so we will have an anger management exercise?

Seth - If you insist.

Mark - It's only because every time I drive to my office I get a little frustrated.

Seth - You need a little tool to take to work with you?

Mark - Yes I do. I think other people will enjoy it too. Particularly since 9/11... everyone's anger level has sky-rocketed.

Anger, Fear and Racism

Mark - Can you just talk about anger, fear, and racism a bit?

Seth - I have dealt with some of that already and I will go deeper into that if you wish. As I stated before, races evolved… the colors of the skin, for instance, evolved because of the climates, the pigments were necessary. We talked about that already. Yesterday I mentioned how the various cultural ideas with mankind's expression of his free will and freedom of his consciousness set up his cultures and then migrated them throughout the planet each time the beliefs being changed a little bit here and there to suit the ones in power. Do I need to elaborate further on that?

Mark - I don't think so, no. I'm just trying to see what the pieces of the book are going to be.

Seth - I will cover this extensively in the book. You've got mass beliefs systems of species of people that appear to be set in stone. They've been passed down from generation to generation as truths, never even being questioned as to why they're there. No one has ever bothered to say, "Wait a minute, why is that?" With the awakening of mankind in your timeframe, he is now starting to question these beliefs. He is learning that his power is within himself, not within others. If he constantly believes that he needs to transfer his power to others, he will not further the evolution of his soul, he will simply give others what is rightfully his.

****

More on Sending Energy
to Simultaneous Lives

Mark - Could you talk a little bit about how you would go about sending energy out to your current life in the past? Healing the past is what I'm getting at here.

Seth - Are you saying your present life when you were a child?

Mark - Yes.

Seth - It matters not to the time space continuum for it only exists on the physical planes. The present will be no different because you are in the Now at this moment. There is no past or future in this moment there is just Now. What you do Now creates those so called pasts and futures. Every part of your being is going to receive that message: past, present and future. The very idea that you are focusing on those thoughts in your present point of power will automatically affect, say, the childhood. You cannot erase what you have experienced in the childhood, but the message in that timeframe is received. So for instance, you're sending thoughts of love, of spirituality, harmonious thoughts for your psychic abilities, mental stability, all of those things are received. In that point in time, your self is unaware that the thoughts are coming through, however they are being received. Your future selves, in the same reference, are sending messages to you as we speak that you are not aware of, the same with your past. The very idea that you are visualizing your thoughts to all of your simultaneous lives is enough to effect the change and to put the message across to those lives. They receive the information, like I said, whether or not they are aware of it. In doing so, closing one's eyes and visualizing that fan spread that I drew up and just sending your energies to all of your simultaneous lives, whether or not you understand the complexity of the process. The fact that you are sending the thought is good enough. It is beyond your comprehension in the third-dimensional reality to understand how this works. That's why I have kept it as simple as possible to use a simple visualization of a thought landing somewhere in your imagination on those lives. Many readers are not aware of those lives, so to them it will be up to their imagination to bring forth information relating to those. Oftentimes your imagination is quite aware of previous lives and will be able to direct for you without you being aware of it. Does that help further clarify?

Mark - It sure does.

Wonders of the Fourth Dimension

Mark - I do have another question related to private material you just spoke about concerning the changes in society, the way we're going to be transporting ourselves, new sources of energy. I've been thinking lately about the scientific world and our technicians and our engineers. It seems that if they were to take your information to heart, they could make breakthroughs in all the different fields. Is that what's going to happen here in the next few years?

Seth - It will eventually. Let me explain something here about the fourth dimension. As mankind moves into the unity of consciousness dimension many of his abilities are enhanced. These things will come naturally as this process takes place. Man will learn to understand the power of his own energy and how to harness his own energy and thought process, to alter his thought process, to alter his environment. The reason you do not have this ability now, is because in the third dimension there are those who would abuse it. This knowledge is obtained only when one has purified their thoughts and successfully made the transition. It is very simple and as the planet moves forward all will become common knowledge. Most of this is hard to comprehend in your three-dimensional reality, however many of you are not going to be in that reality forever. You are definitely moving toward the peaceful fourth dimension. Beings of Light are making great strides to awaken mankind to his energy field, because as you begin understand it you will be able to raise the vibrational hum of your being, thus allowing for the transition. Crystals are highly effective in capturing energy and will be looked at seriously as a source of

power, however the technology will not be given until mankind's thoughts are purified. There are also other sources of free power available to your world after you have made the transition into the fourth-dimensional awareness. The Earth can no longer sustain the primitive methods that mankind uses to propel himself around.

Mark - These crystals, are they the natural crystals that are mined on this planet?

Seth - They are and they are fully capable of harnessing the energy from the sun and beings as well. You will only see them and have access to them in the fourth dimension

Mark - Is this done the same way that a shaman from a traditional culture uses crystals to heal and to help the tribe?

Seth - It's a more primitive way, however the concept has some associations. In the future, the crystals will be quite large and hold massive amounts of energy that will be propelled through grids for the various needs of mankind.

Mark - This sounds like the Atlantean technologies that are talked about in the metaphysical literature.

Seth - It "will" be the reality in the future of your world. Envision the crystals, they are like giant monoliths. All energy can be harnessed within them and re-dispersed.

Mark - And the giant crystals are transmitters and the people will be able to receive the energy in their homes through receivers of some kind?

Seth - The crystals are used to harness the energy. They come in various sizes. The largest ones are used to harness mass amounts of energy. The smaller ones are used for devices which mankind will choose to use in his existence. Again they are not visible to you at this time but you will see them and use them when you cross over into the fourth dimension.

Natural Health

Mark - Cas and I were just talking about how the healthcare system is changing. People are not satisfied with modern medicine, with just taking drugs. They're turning to natural ways of healing, alternative therapies and such. Is that the way we're going to go?

Seth - It is true. Drugs inhibit the natural healing processes of the body. They only mask the problem. They do not remove it. This goes much deeper than the drugs though, because as mankind changes his systems of belief he will see that drugs are no longer effective. He will not need drugs, he will not think he needs drugs, and he will not be standing in line like at the candy store waiting for the latest miracle cure because he will know that the cure is within his own power of his being and that drugs are not a cure. There is no drug on your planet that is a cure. It is simply a mask of symptoms which can only be tolerated for so long before new symptoms appear, then the rotating cycle of a new drug is given and so on and so forth. As mankind moves into the fourth dimension, none of this will be necessary. Humanity will be able to live as many as two-hundred or more years per life cycle unless you meet with accidents. But in this process humanity will also be creating less of its own species, for humanity will not see the need to prolifically populate the planet. You will be free of your guilt related to your sexuality and religious indoctrinations relating to procreation. Earth is moving out of the third-dimensional reality and as this happens there will be no need for some of the archaic habits and beliefs that you have for so long held onto.

Enlightening Mankind
Earthquakes

Mark - Are you able to reveal specific information about the future?

Seth - When I am dictating this book, much information has to be left out. Yet in a way it is very pertinent to your world situation. I am bound by the Laws of Noninterference. However I do not want this reading to come across as something from outer space, so to speak. But outer space is where we all are. Your society does not understand that, so we cannot go in that direction as much as I would like to. Many of your buildings, especially your ancient ones, come from memories of other dimensions, many of the Greek temples, pyramids etc. These were all bleedthroughs of mankind's memory that were recreated on Earth. Some of these, as in the pyramids, have a specific function with relation to your evolution. I will elaborate on this further at some point in your future. Mankind is only using a small portion of his abilities in his creative process on your planet, but you are always and forever creating. Again I say "his" here because of the belief systems of your society and the connotations that are put upon male vs. female ideas. I wish to stay within the framework of that belief system at present because I realize your beliefs will not change overnight. It will be a slow process. So we will use those terms with respect to your beliefs, not mine, for there is no distinction at all. Male or female it makes no difference. You are all souls and soul has no gender. The physical body is merely a vehicle for expression and communication that you have chosen to experience your lives.

Mark - It will be a slow process?

Seth - In your terms, in your frame of time, in time as you know it, as these things don't happen overnight. Now mankind is rapidly moving into his spiritual evolution and is becoming more and more aware every day of the true nature of his existence. But this is unheard of in the millions of years of your evolution. It is necessary to speed up your evolution so that all of you will be able to make it into the fourth dimension. At this time in your twenty-first century, you are able to see the results of this as mankind is more open in his mind to learning about himself than he ever was before. He is moving in the right direction and our efforts have not been in vain for we are seeing the results with many of you. You are not doomed and gloomed for hellfire and damnation. Only a small percentage of the populace will not move into the unity of consciousness dimension. That cannot be helped because there are those who will not seek the light no matter what they are told. They will hang onto their materialistic old ways for dear life although it will not be much of a life when the rest of the planet has moved into the fourth dimension and they are left behind to embrace the materialistic entrapments of the third dimension along with all of its fears and negativity. Most of mankind is striving as we speak to move in that direction, whether they are consciously aware of it or not.

Now Mark, you know you are able to receive thoughts from me. You are aware of those thoughts coming to you. The rest of mankind is also receiving thoughts. Some are aware and some are not. The majority are just beginning their awakening. They know that something is changing their system of beliefs. They're not sure what it is but they feel the change happening. Beings like myself have had a tremendous amount of input into your species at present, because we have all participated in the creation and survival of your beautiful Earth and do not want to see it destroyed by the use of nuclear weapons. That is your greatest threat at present along with your abuse of the ecological systems that were created to keep the planet stable.

Mark - Can you talk some about Earthquakes? Is this nature's way of giving its citizens a gentle reminder?

Seth - You know earthquakes are Earth's way of shifting her skin and giving mankind subtle warnings that she will not tolerate your flagrant abuses of her.

Mark - Do you anticipate any stern, violent reminders that the Earth would experience coming up in the near future?

Seth - I am not allowed to disclose that information due to the Laws of Noninterference and also because even if I did know something it is only a probable reality. Earthquakes say, in California where there is an active fault line, are almost predictable at certain times of year. There is a system of beliefs that after a rainy season there will be movement, and there usually is because it is anticipated. The big April 1906 Earthquake left within the minds of the citizens of that region the possibility that the spring would always bring more Earthquakes and has been a belief for sometime amongst the masses in that area. It would be hard to change that thinking since mankind creates these Earthquakes to reinforce those beliefs. It is not hard to understand then why they happen. And of course you'll have your oh-so-knowledgeable scientists inject their interpretation of the event and do their forecasting thus preparing mankind for the next one. If you look back at the most recent big Earthquake in California, the one called Loma Prieta, you can easily see that it was projected long before it happened. Systematically, through the media the so-called "big one" was on its way any day. As people subscribed to those beliefs they manifested its reality. There could be others depending on what your media decides to put into the minds of your species. Earth on her own also likes to take care of herself with messages to humanity to stop destroying the precious outer and inner layers of her being. Oftentimes Earthquakes can be one or a combination of both depending on the situation and the information being plugged into the minds of mankind.

Names of God

Mark - How will you be referring to god in this book since there are so many names for god?

Seth - I wish to make a point that All That Is encompasses all those names. The readers should understand that their version of god, whatever they call him or her, is encompassed in All That Is. All That Is is an infinite high-energy source. It is impossible for that mass of energy to contain itself into one specific life form. Not even for a minute is it capable of doing this. You are all, we are all I should say, extensions of All That Is in that we use this energy source to experience our lives and as we evolve so does All That Is. Every thought, every action, every feeling, every situation, every moment in time and space is different with each individual. No two people or beings will ever experience the exact situation in the exact same way. All That Is is experiencing what it has created in every way possible, thus expanding its abilities as well as yours, for All That Is is always acquiring more and more knowledge of itself through the existence of souls throughout the Universes, not just your limited little Universe that you are aware of but there are thousands of galaxies just like yours in the infinite amount of space.

Fear
Holographic Inserts

Mark - Can you talk a little further about fear and death, as we think of these concepts?

Seth - If you notice, the problems in your society all revolve around fear, one of those fears being fear of the unknown. If you as a species are to evolve and lose your fears then a willingness to expand your consciousness and to understand the true nature of your being would be in order, especially when it comes to your death the way you perceive it. It's a hard cycle to break the religious dogma that has been so diligently drummed into the minds of man. But without the erasure of some of those beliefs, you are not going to be able to move forward into the next dimension. You know as I talked about the terrorizing of humanity, it comes in many forms under many guises. But when you break it down, it's all related to man's fears, mainly his fear of death. He does not need to be in such fear of his death, for truly he experienced more trauma in his birth than he will ever experience in his death. He needs to accept the reality of his soul's existence and move forward. I cannot stress this enough, how death is not final, the way that you see it. He also needs to take back the power that is rightfully his and stop allowing others to make decisions for him, for his life is to be experienced by him alone, for his soul's evolution. He has been blindly following the ideas of others without questioning them.

The Christian manuscripts leave out reincarnation altogether. Many of you do not question this information about death because it does not correlate with your current manuscripts. However these manuscripts were written by men and altered by men many times over. Jesus, one of the Ascended Masters who mentally and physically shared his body with The Christ entity, did not write your bible/manuscript, men wrote it, with man's interpretations of events the way man saw fit to put them on paper. This entity did not sit there and write these words for you, yet you believe that he did through the writings of others. Much of the messages that The Christ entity brought forward were never even put into your manuscripts.

Now, in getting back to fear, the negative forces are banking on mankind's fears. The disruptions that they cause feed them a steady diet of negativity which allows them to grow. You will be able to dis-empower them by not buying into it in the first place. I know you will say this is hard to do and it is hard to do because of the biological responses associated with the physical vehicle when put in a situation of threat or peril. If you understand that you are really not in a perilous situation at all, you will be better equipped to confront situations without fear and use your innate survival instincts to survive the situation. However, if you were unable to rise above this feeling, know that if you do shed your body, you did so because you had planned this for yourself, it was one of the many probabilities for your death. When you choose to manifest one of those probabilities, this is the death that you will experience. All of you have gone through life encountering many situations where that probable death could have been manifested but you chose not to. When you are ready you will choose and when you are not you will survive your experience. Sometimes you come so close, but then there is a lesson to be given in that experience. Sometimes the lesson will alter the way you live the rest of your life either physically, mentally, emotionally or spiritually. And you may say, "My loved one wasn't ready, my loved one was living their life, my loved one was happy." True, this may be so. You may want to look a little further and see if that loved one experienced his death or her death for you to experience another situation in your life where you needed to grow and learn. It will help you to understand that all of these probable realities have been worked out in the beginning when you set up your lives with all of the souls that you incarnate with. If you understand this concept it will be much easier for you to let go when you need to and to also experience your life more fully. Experience the everyday pleasures of your life that you would normally deny yourself because of your fears. For within these experiences there is a wealth of information and learning that is available to you to further the evolution of your soul.

If you allow yourself to accept the reality of the nature of your soul you will find that the terrorists have no power, because you have effectively removed it from them by not succumbing to the fear. The dark forces have been fighting to have the planet Earth as their home base. Beings of Light will not allow this to happen for Earth was never intended to be a base for the dark forces. Earth itself is moving out of its third-dimensional reality and the forces of dark will be unable to sustain themselves in its new dimension. They are in the process of being sealed-off to their own dimension. However at this point in your time they still have the ability to influence you. If you allow the dark forces to manipulate your thoughts and feed off of the negativity that is created and the anxiety that you physically feel, you are serving them up a sumptuous buffet of everything that they desire. For if they can kill the hope and the love within the souls of mankind, they have won. Dis-empower them by embracing fear with love, a love for each other, and a love for your planet and all living creatures. They will stop terrorizing the world if the world no longer is in fear of them and takes charge of the destiny of all souls to move forward into the fourth dimension, using many of the tools that I have written of in this book. Your governments and media should be using the communication devises that they have created for the good of mankind rather than feeding the negative forces. You can change all of this so easily if you come together as one and stand up and expose the negative forces for who they are. For in doing so each one of you will start to raise your vibrational hum and move into the light and all the knowledge that is available to you.

Good and Evil

Mark - What do you think of our ideas of good and evil? Some people here consider those who do not conform to their way of thinking as evil. How do you see it?

Seth - You have your version of good and evil but in reality there is no good or evil, it is just an experience and sometimes a misguided one at that, but nonetheless it is an experience, a balancing of negative and positive for the evolution of the soul. But when looking at your ideas of evil it all comes back to the negative forces wishing to control the minds of mankind. They are part of a balancing of the experiences of this planet but they are now out of control and have disrupted the divine plan of The Creator. They have enslaved you into engulfing yourselves in the trappings of materialism. The citizens of the nations of wealth and power are all consumed by their materialistic desires and have forgotten the true purpose of their soul. Negative influences will use whatever means necessary to keep this planet from moving into the peaceful fourth dimension and that will not be tolerated by The Creator. At this time in your world, they are causing small little wars in many countries around the world. They are also deeply entrenched in forcing the poorer nations to succumb to the will of political and corporate greed. It would behoove you to become more consciously aware of this and look to your leaders and demand that they help these nations as they struggle with the influx of corporate greed and terrorist infiltration. If you do not see the need of humanity as it is so obvious, then you do so by choice and you are not evolving.

It is ultimately your decision as to whether you want to let the forces of dark prevail because of your unwillingness to get involved or whether you will take a stand for the rights of humanity and help your brothers now. As I said before, we will interfere if necessary but we are limited as to how much we can interfere. The Universal Law allows for us to interfere in certain situations but even these situations are highly scrutinized by Hierarchy. Do not think that we are going to show up and save the day for it is up to mankind to do this on his own. We will simply not allow the planet to be destroyed. The lessons will still have to be learned by man one-by-one. It is not inconceivable to see as many as thirty million of you succumb in the near future. It is a probable reality of your own doing if it happens. And it will be a learning experience for all of mankind for it may be your next wake-up call to realign your consciousness. It is a critical time in the history of the planet Earth. Your reality as you know it now is coming to a close. All of you have the ability individually and collectively to make the transition a peaceful one. Uniting your thoughts and beliefs in alignment with the true nature of you-the-soul and focusing on a peaceful oneness with the rest of humanity by removing the separation of yourself with others will make it happen. It is time for you in the nations of power to share the resources of your planet with other nations that have nothing or very little instead of hogging all the resources for yourselves. It is also critical that you start to clean up your environment from the toxic cyclone of chemicals and radiation that you surround yourselves with. This must be done if you are to survive as a species. Do you have any questions?

Mark - I always have questions.

Seth - It saddens me to see what humans have been able to do to each other. It shouldn't have to be this way.

Mark - Well sometimes humans have to be frightened into changing.

Seth - They do and more than once. But the point is not to instill fear in humanity, but to stimulate their thoughts so that they will be consciously aware. Until those thoughts that they produce are in alignment with the will of The Creator they will continue to experience their current level of negativity and will not further the evolution of their souls into your next dimension of awareness.

Mark - It seems that sometimes it has to be a matter of life and death before people do change in any meaningful way.

Seth - I'm trying to avoid that by giving them a sense of their death and the acceptance of it and what it means as well as their beliefs about their reality. Thoughts are so powerful and you still do not get that message as yet. Your negative thoughts are still running rampant throughout the Universe and it is slowing down your evolution. I cannot emphasize enough to you how important your thoughts are and how important it is to keep them pure and loving. Your thoughts are what will determine your future and whether you as a species survive on your planet.

Humans are a very stubborn bunch. Years ago I spoke of your thoughts and how they could change your reality and yet many of you have forgotten and have slipped back into your old ways. That was a primer then to get you moving, but you have not moved much. Now your time is almost up and I am trying once again to stimulate you into realigning your thoughts and beliefs. This may be old material to some of you, but many of you have fallen back to sleep. This time if you fall asleep you may be left behind. It is up to you. For you and only you are the ones who can make that decision. You have free will. I can give you all the tools you need, however if you don't use them, that is your choice.

Mark -You talked earlier about holographic inserts. What is a holographic insert?

Seth - Yes, we will discuss holographic inserts for there are many in the history of the world. In order to broaden the horizons of the minds of man, or to awaken him with a mass lesson, holographic inserts are often used as an illusional effect. Holographic inserts can be used any time Hierarchy gives its approval to create a mass event that didn't really happen. Now I know some readers are going to have difficulty with this but nonetheless, this is real. I will not give any instances of their use for it is not necessary. You may also use a holographic insert between lives to go through a chosen portal to view a life you wish to enter into. It's very simple. By entering through that portal you may go in and observe one of the many life experiences you have set up for yourself and view different events going on in that life and decide for yourself whether or not you wish to experience this life in this timeframe. Generally between lives you may enter three or four different lives searching for the one that you feel would be most beneficial to the evolution of your soul and you do this through the use of holographic inserts. These lives are taking place whether it is your soul entering into the body or that of another. You will determine with your free will what the experiences and outcome of the choices made in the life of that body entail. Most often the body will be created whether it is inhabited by your soul or that of another. Through the hologram you are getting a glimpse of the conditions of that reality. You will make your decision based on whether or not you are ready to enter into that mass belief system and its conditions at that time or not. Now mankind creates most of what he perceives in his world. He does create his reality, but this reality can be altered in many ways. When interference needs to be used for the benefit of mankind, we are perfectly capable of assisting with the holographic inserts. There have been several mass events throughout your world's history that were holographically created. For now I will leave it at that.

Relationships

Mark - Do you think people will actually make an effort to change or will they just keep on with business as usual?

Seth - Most of you if you consciously question your beliefs will not have a hard time digesting this material. There are a few things in the material that are futuristic which I am able to talk about without going into too much detail and I don't believe there is anything in there that is going to hurt anyone. It will stimulate the readers to look at their system of beliefs and to question once again why they have them and to understand why it is important to love one another regardless of their chosen package, for that is all it is, a package or vehicle with which you are able to experience and communicate with each other. You have all taken it to the extreme though and distorted it into a false reality of a destructive nature.

The message throughout the Universe is love and cooperation with one another. We do it freely. It is only you humans who have a problem with it. This book is material to try to stimulate you into conquering your fears and rethinking and realigning your beliefs. Mankind has continuously put obstacles in front of his own enlightenment over and over again but this is not entirely of his own doing. Again it comes back to the dark forces and the level of manipulation that they have attained.

If you look at it from the view of Beings of Light, who are in alignment with the will and divine purpose of The Creator and All That Is, you will begin to understand. There is so much more to experience in your world that would bring you into the light. Have you ever noticed how good you feel when you've given love to another unselfishly. All of you could be walking around in a state of ecstasy if you chose to do so. There is no drug in your world as powerful as the soul's love. That feeling is euphoric. Instead of subscribing to the fear-based dogma of all of your institutions that you have created for yourself, why not create the heavenly bliss of your soul's true nature. You can do this. It is not impossible. It is a matter of redirecting your energies inward and bringing forth your soul-light. What has been created can be undone as you are all co-creators of your Universe.

Mark - The idea of experiencing ecstasy all the time?

Seth - All the time.

Mark - Well that's always been part of my journey, trying to find out how I can do that and then teaching other people how to do that. Is it possible for me to connect people to that in my practice?

Seth - Everyone can do this and when they do, they will not forget. Try it out on yourself. Do things for strangers. Give them money. Buy their groceries. Simple acts of kindness to others is a way to start feeling the joy that your soul came here to feel. Most often you are going to get a positive reaction from those that you express kindness to. For one, they're not going to be expecting it.

Mark - That's for sure (humorously)

Seth - And number two, when they get it, it's going to change their attitude and they may pass that along to someone else and thus starts the curve of mankind learning to trust and to appreciate his fellow man. You have yourself in such a rut where you don't trust each other and it's not entirely your fault because the negative forces have been at play ensuring that you fear each other, that you fear love, that you fear closeness, that you'll be hurt, that you'll be destroyed, that you'll be tramped on, and so you must withdraw into your shell and hope that no one can touch you, no one can get into the hard little shell that you've encased yourself in and you go through life all wrapped up in a little cocoon trying to burst out, but each time you burst out you get bombarded with your fears and then you retreat back into your cocoon again. And you think, if I can just make it through I'll be OK. Humans are very open and willing to accept love if it's given freely and unconditionally. They have a problem with the conditions, for they always feel that if a person does a kindness for them that there's going to be a condition, there's going to be an attachment. They are going to have to provide something of themselves that they are usually unwilling to do. This does not have to be so. You can move in the direction of love without expecting anything in return except for the joy that it gives your soul-You, to have given to another. That in itself is more reward than anything else.

You must all learn to love each other while in the physical bodies of the third dimension while being exposed to the constant bombardment of the forces of dark. This is something you are supposed to master while in incarnation. It is the soul's purpose to reflect itself through its vehicle the body. When you have accomplished this, you move out of the physical body and into the etheric. You all DO love each other. When you are not in your dense physical bodies that are weighted down by the gravitational forces of the Earth and your spirit is freely moving about in your etheric body throughout the Universe in your dreams, you love each other. It's just when you come back into the physical reality that you put up the roadblocks. Earth is a school of hard knocks but it does not have to be so. It is your creation and it stems from your beliefs about who you are, a creation that you have willing subscribed to because you have handed over your power to others. You have not taken charge of your lives in a way that would allow for your evolution in a peaceful and harmonious way. You could easily recreate Earth to be a paradise, a heaven so-called on Earth. It is totally within your capability to do so, yet most of you choose to cling to the fear and the terror and the negativity.   The stimulation that you crave is right there at your fingertips, it does not have to come from negative dark thoughts. Thoughts and actions of love can produce the same results. You have become addicted to the flow of your own adrenaline. But what you are trying to do is capture the feelings from your soul memories, the euphoric feelings that are based on your love for each other and a oneness with All That Is, the feelings you have forgotten in your cosmic slumber that are now ready to awaken if you let them.

(this last piece of material was delivered so quickly I had a difficult time keeping up with the typing)

Laws of Noninterference

Mark - You mentioned the Laws of Noninterference, you can't be more specific about what's going on? What are the Laws of Noninterference?

Seth - I am not at liberty to change or alter the destiny of mankind. I am allowed to give information that will prompt the minds of man to think and respond, however it is not my purpose to guide you by the hand step-by-step and tell you what to do in any situation. The purpose of incarnating to your planet is for the soul to grow and experience within its own nature without any interference from outside sources. Otherwise why bother to experience Earth life? We have been interfering somewhat lately because of the disarray of the planet. The impending shift into the fourth dimension is upon you. You as a species were not ready and that is why I am communicating with you. I am one of many who have spoken to humans about what needs to be done to survive the shift. The time has come once again to alert you to your reality because time as you know it is coming to a close in this chapter of your evolution. The transition into the peaceful fourth dimension requires a certain level of evolution to happen successfully. It is happening whether you are ready or not. It is my purpose and that of others to get you ready quickly for you have lingered far too long in the realms of darkness.

Soul Age

Mark - Is it OK to ask a question to begin?

Seth - Absolutely.

Mark - Cas and I were just wondering about the terms "soul age, young souls, old souls." Do you think in terms of that in the way you see things? Is there sort of a hierarchy there?

Seth - It is not considered a hierarchy when you are talking about the age of a soul. Give me a moment here and I will explain. Old souls simply have incarnated many times. When you consider an old soul, you are thinking that soul should be wiser and more experienced, however this is not always the case. An old soul can also be a soul who has failed to learn their lessons and continuously comes back for another go at it. Therefore, there is no real logic to using the term old soul with the idea of attributing more wisdom to it. New souls are exactly that. These souls usually are first-time incarnations into the physical body of Earth. They're somewhat like babies. You can recognize them usually by their childish and somewhat unsure behaviors. They move around like children playing in a fairyland. Life to them is not very serious and they don't see it as a serious thing, it is more of a fun and games. This sometimes can get them into a world of trouble for they are unprepared to use the skills that others have acquired to maneuver through the physical plane. A lot of new souls, because they have not incarnated before and their needs have always been taken care of in their home dimension, come to your world and cannot understand why their needs are not automatically taken care of. They have a hard time with the negativity on your planet, for they remember far better than most, the way it is in the soul's home dimension where love for one another is automatic. Let's just put it this way, after many more incarnations they will start to get the picture of what a third-dimensional reality with the influences of the forces of dark is all about. They will then have to make the decision as to how fast they wish to evolve because evolution on the planet Earth is much harder than other planets due to the negativity. However, some of these entities will only come to the Earth plane one time and then choose to move on to somewhere else where it is easier for them. Eventually though all will have to experience the negativity associated with the third-dimensional planes whether on Earth or elsewhere if they wish to further their evolution. It is entirely up to you as to how fast or slow you wish to progress and truly it makes no difference how long you wish to take. There is a certain level of stimulation within your soul groups that prompts you to move forward. Because you are living in a dimension that provides for all your needs when you are not incarnated, it is easy for you to forget how tough

Earth can be. Many of you will bite off more than you can chew even though you have been advised not to do so. Most of you have incarnated many times, so therefore you are living many lives simultaneously, learning from each one of them as you go. Does that clarify that for you?

Mark - It sure does. Thank you for that.

Experiencing the Fourth Dimension

Mark - I'm still curious about the move into the unity of consciousness dimension. Could you clarify what's going to happen as the transition is completed?

Seth - Yes let me go into this further. Earth is evolving into the fourth dimension of peace, as I stated earlier. It is the unity of consciousness dimension. You are being awakened so that you will be able to stay in this dimension because controlling your thoughts will be the key to you being able to stay there. If you are not ready, you will not be able to stay there. The knowledge is being given to mankind to make the necessary changes in his life patterns to move along with the planet into this dimension. The planet is still going to be there, but not in the way that you currently are experiencing it. The fourth dimension refers to a level of awareness and thoughts are instantly manifested into reality. If you create fears for yourself and you actualize those fears and say kill someone, you will not be able to stay. This is why I am writing again to try to stimulate you into becoming consciously aware of what you think and believe. This will determine who stays and who does not because thoughts of negativity are not allowed there. Most likely you won't be walking down the street one day and all of a sudden "be there," but then again, it could happen this way. Since this is an unprecedented evolution in the way it will be experienced, no one surely knows just how it will take place. Because of other mitigating factors in your world, it will not happen as it has in the past. It is truly an event that all are watching in my dimension and others. It's a process that's taking place as we sit here and it is constantly evolving itself. We are diligently putting forth the information to your species to realign your thoughts and to understand why it is necessary to do so.

Now, there will always be some of you who will refuse, and that is where, as I said earlier, that when the transition of their energy from the physical third dimension is manifested in their next incarnation, they will have to incarnate within the third-dimensional realms where they will be with minds like their own. It is important because Earth and all the planets in your solar system are moving into higher dimensions at this time. I am also in the process of a grand evolution myself. You have free will to choose, but as this planet moves forward you will not go with it. You will when the time comes have to resurface in the same reality which you have created for yourself on Earth. Many, many of you are happily moving into a new alignment with All That Is and consciously becoming aware of your thoughts and the way they affect your entire Universe. We have moved much information into your books and the media through the use of movies and many of you have accepted it and are diligently trying to lead better, more aware lives. This will continue until such time that it is no longer necessary.

Psychics, Mediums and Channels

Mark - I heard a parapsychologist on the radio the other day who was talking about the distinctions that he felt there were between mediums, psychics and channelers.

Seth - It is all fodder for thought.

Mark - It IS all fodder for thought. I tend to believe that there are not really distinctions. I mean they're all just names.

Seth - There is no distinction.

Mark - OK now there was also this fellow on TV talking to the deceased. Can you elaborate on that?

Seth - It's all in relation to how you focus your abilities. Some will focus on the psychic realms while others will focus more on speaking to souls who are on the Astral Plane. All of you are capable of all three. You have an uncanny way of trying to put things into little boxes. For some reason you feel that if it is contained in a box with a title you are able to understand it better. Your limited perception of reality necessitates this for you.

Mark - To add to that last question, this fellow who was on TV, he was talking to the departed loved-ones of celebrities. Can you comment on that?

Seth - He is able to tap into the dimension of the Astral Plane. This is not hard to do. Any one of you could do this. Humanity is constantly trying to reassure itself of its own ideas of its mortality. It takes a willingness to listen and be able to decipher the voices of those with which you wish to communicate. That is all. It is quit easy. It is to focus your attention in that arena of communication and be able to filter out outside stimulation and distractions. It is a very high level of meditation in a way because the person wishing to communicate must exhibit a certain level of discipline within his being. But it is a very attainable state for all of you. There is no mystery to it.

Mark - That's basically what the program was about.

Seth - An edited version at that. Had you seen the entire transcript, there were also many errors. Not necessarily errors on his part, but between the communication of the subjects and the entities. Realize that entities in the Astral Plane use a form of symbols and clues. They're not very adept at

241

communicating. It is up to the entity receiving the information to clarify what he or she is hearing. The higher dimensions of the Astral Plane are a waiting and learning area. Many times when communicating with a so-called medium, the information that appears to be logical to the entity in waiting does not always make it through in that format. It can come in somewhat distorted at times. This is not rocket science you know. It is a very easy thing for all of mankind to do. It's just a matter of focusing and listening. Often the problem lies in the area of too many entities wanting to speak to the medium at the same time. As I said before, they are not very good at this and tend to want to jump in and be heard and there lies the confusion. Many of you do not want to communicate because of your fears and religious indoctrination. It is easy to do, but if you do not believe in it, it serves no purpose.

The Crumbling of Oppressive Organizations

Seth - Do you have any questions?

Mark - Well yes. I've got several thousand here.

Seth - I had the feeling you did.

Mark - Yes, all the material is evocative and so that makes me think about questions. OK there's a broad question I have. Our belief systems, in the form of religions, like Catholicism, are crumbling?

Seth - The oppression of mankind is crumbling away piece by piece.

Mark - And this is part of the process of moving Earth into the unity of consciousness dimension?

Seth - Mankind will come to terms with its own soul and realize that he doesn't have to be dominated or guilt-ravaged by the idea manipulations of others. The guilt-ridden ideas that have been injected into your belief system have essentially delayed the evolution of your soul. You saw a return or a resurgence of people going back to church after 9/11. Now you see the fall of the church because this was not the answer. The answer lies in your ability to open up your own self to your realities that you have created, to understand that everything around you was created by you. You cannot put the blame somewhere else when it lies in your own backyard. You cannot run to God and expect it to be fixed for you. You became scared. You were faced with your own perceived mortality and because of your beliefs it terrified you. Your thoughts, your ideas, your perceived realities create and did create your reality as you know it. If you want the reality of your world to change you will have to start with yourself. An inner examination of self through meditation will help you start to change your reality. There are many of us out there awakening you. You are being awakened as to the true nature of your soul's existence. As I have said before and will say again, underlined Mark, <u>You are a soul with a body, not a body with a soul.</u> You have thought of yourself as a body with a little soul tucked away somewhere in the recesses of your mind to sometimes be brought out on Sundays when you go to church and then neatly tucked back away in that little box you have created, giving all credit to the body and the ego for your existence when in actuality that is not the case. Your body again, is simply a vehicle for expression and communication. Without you-the-soul maneuvering it, it would be like a comatose person. It would function but there would not be any communication of life force mentally, emotionally or spiritually. It would just be a body, physically functioning, that is it.

Mark - I'm trying to see what the dynamic is here. We're fighting back against oppression and then this causes more oppression?

Seth - The oppression stems from the knowledge that you inherently as a soul know and what has been systematically indoctrinated into your thought process. You are in a constant struggle from what you know to be true and what others, the ones in power, the manipulators, want you to believe. You cannot fool yourself. Even though you try to rationalize your reality, you-the-soul knows different. It only causes more oppression because you have two perceived realities fighting for the right to be heard and expressed: the true reality of the soul and the reality of the ego-self. As you move away from the systematic indoctrination of fear and guilt-ridden religious ideas and put the ego in its place, the oppression will subside. I am not putting down your churches, however the information that they give you has not seemed to help. It has only hindered your very soul's evolution. If you are constantly feeling guilty or bad about the existence of your self, how can you possibly move further ahead towards the light if you do not feel worthy of that light? This is where the oppression comes in. As you know, most churches have strict rules about your behaviors and experiences that your soul is allowed to have. I am not advocating running out and perpetrating crimes against humanity because all of a sudden you feel you have the right to, because you do not and will certainly be in violation of Universal Law. I am saying examine your beliefs, look at the information that is being given to you. Does it allow you to move closer to the light of The Creator, or does it further repress your soul into a guilt-ridden fear? That reality that is created for you, that fear-based reality, is what you have accepted as the norm.

As you awaken, you will understand that fear is at the root of most of your problems: fear to acknowledge who you are, fear of each other, fear of confronting your own perceived reality, fear of acknowledging your soul's existence, fear of everything that does not conform to your limited perceptions of your own isolated reality. You would rather stay comfortable in your thought process where you don't have to accept this responsibility and can shirk it off to someone else. Oh, leave it up to the pastor. I shall go in and confess my sins and absolve myself and get on with my life, business as usual. This does not work. You have not moved anywhere by doing so. You are still stuck in the same perceived reality that you were in when you walked in. Any more questions? Would you like a break to write them down?

Mark - Well I have a question right now. I know many Catholics who, even though the institution is obviously crumbling, still maintain that they're going to stick with it to the bitter end.

Seth - To the bitter end, notice how they have said "bitter" end. It will take a great awakening on the part of the churches to admit what they have been doing to the masses. But since they have not been willing to do it in the past, an intervention was necessary and you are in the midst of it as we speak. I will leave it at that. You see the crumbling of one church but when you look at it, the crumbling of the Muslim religion is in the same throes. Religion is not meant to be what it is now. It was not meant to repress the people. It was not meant to instill so much fear into the people that they could not live their lives and experience their soul's evolution. This was never the intention. When The Christ essence appeared in the many forms that he has appeared in, it was never to do what organized religions have done to the belief systems of mankind. As you know, I have stated The Christ essence is going to come into your world again and he is present now as we speak and has been for over twenty years. He comes with many other Masters to realign the relationships of the people of your world and will stay for some two thousand years. It is not that the Catholic church is going to crumble down completely, nor is any other religious organization. They all are going to be restructured in truth and unity. The Spiritual Hierarchy of your planet is in the process of this realignment now. Old ways must be broken down and truths revealed so that the unification of consciousness can express itself. You are in the midst of a great restructuring of the beliefs of the citizens of your planet. All of your religious organizations will eventually unite together as one truth in alignment with the will and plan of The Creator. I will leave it at that for now.

Realigning Beliefs

Mark - Can you talk about what the average person will experience as they go through the process of realigning their beliefs? It seems to me that you might have a lot of fear.

Seth - The average person right now is saturated almost to the boiling point with fear. The forces of light are already fighting back with your media, vehemently protesting the onslaught of negative and hateful material that is being projected to the masses. You can see this happening. Mankind is in such a state of fear that it is desperately seeking an end to all that it is experiencing in this realm of existence. There are many forces of light in place now and they will be instrumental in exposing the ones who have deceived you and taken advantage of you. You will be experiencing a lot of turmoil within your perceived reality of your most solid beliefs. Beliefs that you have hung onto since birth will start to crumble before you. It is because these things must come to pass before the emergence of the unity of consciousness dimension. There will be a lot of fear. People are going to be confused and torn between the old system of beliefs and the new reality for their world. It will be hard for some to give up the pleasures of the dark forces and turn to the light and alignment with All That Is. They will have to make decisions based on their free will as to which way they choose to go.

If you are listening to your inner self, you should be able to recognize that you are already starting to move into a new level of awareness about your reality. This is happening ever so gently but rapidly right now. Your new reality is in the process of unfolding into your awareness. Soon you will start to abandon your old ways and naturally gravitate towards the light. Your firmest ideas and beliefs will begin to crumble away and you will see no need to hang onto them and will wonder why you ever did. It will be acutely apparent to you what you must do to evolve and you will willingly want to get involved in your world's evolution. There will be a great unity with your brother, an unending love that you have never known in your reality on Earth. It will be a most beautiful thing. As the energies from your Spiritual Hierarchy are poured into your world and begin to manifest themselves in your reality you will become fully awakened and with that you will enter into the next phase of your evolution.

Mark - So that's it. Are you going to tell the reader what that new reality has in store for them?

Seth - For now that is it. I will expand on that reality in my next book.

*I think we're going to have to do a book or two
or three or four or many more to get
the masses to see the problem ...*

MORE BOOKS?

Seth has promised to continue to communicate with us to further the awakening of humanity. This means that there will be an ongoing source of current, inspirational messages available here at:

Seth Returns Publishing

Communications from Seth on the Awakening of Humanity
Volume One *9/11 The Unknown Reality of the World......$19.95*
The first original Seth book in two decades.
Volume Two ....*CALL*
To be published Spring 2004.
Volume Three...*CALL*
To be published Fall 2004.

Available by mail at:

Seth Returns Publishing
P.O. Box 150152 San Rafael, CA 94915-0152 (415) 459-2487
Personal check or money order should include the cost of book plus $5.00 for handling and shipping in the Continental United States and Canada. For delivery elsewhere please call: (415) 459-2487.

Please include 7.25 % sales tax if ordering in California.

You can also shop online at our website: **SethReturns.com**

Expectations p 39

God defined p 220